The publisher John Calder began the Opera Guides series under the editorship of the late Nicholas John in association with English National Opera in 1980. It ran until 1994 and eventually included forty-eight titles, covering fifty-eight operas. The books in the series were intended to be companions to the works that make up the core of the operatic repertory. They contained articles, illustrations, musical examples and a complete libretto and singing translation of each opera in the series, as well as bibliographies and discographies.

The aim of the present relaunched series is to make available again the guides already published in a redesigned format with new illustrations, some newly commissioned articles, updated reference sections and a literal translation of the libretto that will enable the reader to get closer to the intentions and meaning of the original. New guides of operas not already covered will be published alongside the redesigned ones from the old series.

Gary Kahn
Series Editor

Sponsors of the Overture Opera Guides

for the 2015/16 Season at ENO

Norma

Vincenzo Bellini

Overture Opera Guides
Series Editor
Gary Kahn

Editorial Consultant
Philip Reed

OVERTURE

OVERTURE OPERA GUIDES
in association with

EN
O

Overture Publishing
an imprint of

ALMA CLASSICS LTD
3 Castle Yard
Richmond
Surrey TW10 6TF
United Kingdom

Articles by Susan Rutherford, Roger Parker, John Allison and Gary Kahn first published in this volume © the authors, 2016

This *Norma* Opera Guide first published by Overture Publishing, an imprint of Alma Classics Ltd, 2016

© Alma Classics Ltd, 2016
All rights reserved

Translation of libretto © Kenneth Chalmers

Printed in United Kingdom by CPI Group (UK) Ltd, Croydon CR0 4YY

ISBN: 978-1-84749-594-5

Contents

List of Illustrations   8

The Genesis of *Norma*   9
  Susan Rutherford

Norma's Musical Journey   25
  Roger Parker

Norma: A Selective Performance History   42
  John Allison

Weep, Shudder, Die: Vincenzo Bellini, *Norma*   61
  and Their Admirers
  Gary Kahn

Thematic Guide   70

Norma, Libretto   73

    Act One   75

    Act Two   121

Select Discography   166

Norma on DVD   170

Select Bibliography   172

Bellini Websites   174

Note on the Contributors   175

Acknowledgements   176

List of Illustrations

1. Vincenzo Bellini
2. Felice Romani (Museo Teatrale alla Scala)
3. Playbill for the premiere at La Scala
4. La Scala at the beginning of the nineteenth century (Museo Teatrale alla Scala)
5. Stage design for the premiere at La Scala
6. Giuditta Pasta
7. Giuditta Pasta
8. Domenico Donzelli, Giulia Grisi and Giuditta Pasta
9. Domenico Donzelli
10. Vincenzo Negrini
11. Giulia Grisi
12. Maria Malibran
13. Adelaide Kemble
14. Lilli Lehmann (Metropolitan Opera Archives)
15. Rosa Ponselle (Metropolitan Opera Archives)
16. Claudia Muzio
17. Gina Signa (Metropolitan Opera Archives)
18. Zinka Milanov (Metropolitan Opera Archives)
19. Marion Telva (Metropolitan Opera Archives)
20. Giacomo Lauri-Volpi (Metropolitan Opera Archives)
21. Ezio Pinza (Metropolitan Opera Archives)
22. Giovanni Martinelli (Metropolitan Opera Archives)
23. Maria Callas, Catania
24. Maria Callas and Mario Del Monaco, La Scala (Erio Piccagliani)
25. Maria Callas, Opéra de Paris (Roger Pic)
26. Recording session for Maria Callas's first commercial *Norma* (Publicfoto)
27. Callas curtain call, Paris (Roger-Viollet/ArenaPAL)
28. Joan Sutherland (Metropolitan Opera Archives)
29. Marilyn Horne and Joan Sutherland (Ron Scherl/ArenaPAL)
30. Montserrat Caballé
31. June Anderson and Cecilia Díaz (Maximo Parpagnoli)
32. Nelly Miricioiu (Marco Borggreve/Dutch National Opera)
33. Keri Alkema and Annemarie Kremer (Alastair Muir)
34. Cecilia Bartoli (Hans Jörg Michel)
35. Carmela Remigio and Mariella Devia (Rocco Casaluci)
36. Sondra Radvanovsky (Cory Weaver/San Francisco Opera)

1. Vincenzo Bellini, oil portrait (artist unknown)
*c.*1831, the year of the premiere of *Norma*.

2. Felice Romani, the librettist of *Norma*, who worked
with Bellini on eight of his ten operas,
lithograph by Gaetano Cornienti, *c*.1830.

3. Playbill for the premiere of *Norma* at La Scala.

4. La Scala in the early nineteenth century (above).
5. Stage design by Alessandro Sanquirico for the Druid temple
at the premiere of *Norma* at La Scala (below).

6. Giuditta Pasta, the first Norma, oil painting
in character by François Gérard, early 1830s.

The cast of the La Scala premiere: 7. Giuditta Pasta as Norma (top left).
8. Domenico Donzelli as Pollione, Giulia Grisi as Adalgisa and Giuditta Pasta
as Norma (top right). 9. Domenico Donzelli as Pollione (bottom left).
10. Vincenzo Negrini, the first Oroveso (bottom right).

Normas in the nineteenth century: 11. Giulia Grisi, who went on to sing Norma, having sung Adalgisa at the premiere (top left). 12. Maria Malibran, who also sang many leading Rossini roles (top right). 13. Adelaide Kemble, student of Pasta, one of the few English singers to have had success in the role (bottom left). 14. Lilli Lehmann, whose roles also included Isolde and Brünnhilde (bottom right).

Normas in the first half of the twentieth century:
15. Rosa Ponselle (top left). 16. Claudia Muzio (top right).
17. Gina Signa (bottom left).
18. Zinka Milanov (bottom right).

19. Marion Telva as Adalgisa (top left).
20. Giacomo Lauri-Volpi as Pollione (top right).
21. Ezio Pinza as Oroveso (bottom left).
22. Giovanni Martinelli as Pollione (bottom right).

Maria Callas in performance:
23. Teatro Massimo Bellini, Catania, 1950 (above).
24. La Scala 1955, with Mario Del Monaco as Pollione (below).

25. Opéra National de Paris 1964.

26. Recording session for Maria Callas's first commercial *Norma*, 1954, with Nicola Rossi-Lemeni (Oroveso), Rina Cavallari (Clotilde) and Mario Filippeschi (Pollione) (above). 27. Callas curtain call, Opéra National de Paris 1964 (below).

28. Joan Sutherland as Norma at the time of her first
appearances in the role at the Met, 1970 (above).
29. Marilyn Horne as Adalgisa and Joan Sutherland
as Norma at San Francisco Opera, 1982 (below).

30. Montserrat Caballé as Norma in the outdoor Théâtre Antique d'Orange, Provence, 1974 (above). 31. June Anderson as Norma and Cecilia Díaz as Adalgisa in the production directed and designed by Yannis Kokkos at the Teatro Colón, Buenos Aires, in 2001 (below).

32. Nelly Miricioiu in the production directed by Guy Joosten and designed by Johannes Leiacker at Netherlands Opera in 2005 (above). 33. Keri Alkema as Adalgisa and Annemarie Kremer as Norma in the production directed by Christopher Alden, set designed by Charles Edwards and costumes by Sue Willmington, at Opera North in 2012 (below). The production was seen at ENO in 2016.

34. Cecilia Bartoli as Norma in the production directed by Moshe Leiser and Patrice Caurier and designed by Christian Fenouillat first seen at the Salzburg Whitsun Festival in 2013 (above). 35. Carmela Remigio as Adalgisa and Mariella Devia as Norma at the Teatro Comunale, Bologna, in 2013 (bottom left). 36. Sondra Radvanovsky as Norma at San Francisco Opera in 2015 (bottom right).

The Genesis of *Norma*

Susan Rutherford

As 1831 drew to a close, Milan waited with mounting anticipation for the opening of the winter season – the so-called 'carnival' – of theatrical entertainment on 26th December. The city was then in the midst of a feverish epoch dubbed the *'regno delle ballerine'* (the 'reign of the ballerinas') when social life revolved mainly around theatre, opera, ballet and the attendant emergence of a new cult of celebrity. Massimo d'Azeglio – artist, author and politician – later wrote of the 'truly extraordinary sensations' experienced by audiences at those nightly performances.[1] Five theatres, including the puppet theatre, were preparing for the start of the new season, offering Gaetano Fiorio's *L'intollerante* at the Teatro alla Canobbiana (Compagnia Antonio Raftopulo); Francesco Augusto Bon's *Miss Meares, ovvero Un patto ereditario* (inspired by Fanny Burney's novel *Cecilia*) performed by Bon's own company at the Teatro Re; Giuseppe Moncalvo's company at the Teatro Carcano with his skits on the popular Milanese folk character Meneghino; and finally at La Scala the grandest event of all – a new opera by Vincenzo Bellini and the librettist Felice Romani, composed expressly for the soprano Giuditta Pasta and entitled *Norma*.

Throughout operatic history there are works that have been predominantly the result of a composer's inspiration and effort. *Norma*, however, was very much the product of three of the most accomplished operatic talents of their generation: Bellini, Romani and

---

1   Massimo d'Azeglio, *I miei ricordi*, 2 vols. (Florence: G. Barèra, 1869), Vol. II, p. 373.

Pasta. Each brought an artistic vision of notable originality, and their separate paths to that premiere on 26th December illustrate the nature of their individual contributions.

Bellini's Early Career

Born in Sicily in 1801, Bellini had first arrived in Milan in 1827, only two years after graduating from the Conservatorio di San Sebastiano in Naples. Contracted by La Scala's powerful impresario, Domenico Barbaia, Bellini composed his third opera, *Il pirata*, which opened on 24th October 1827 and was praised for its 'simplicity, grace, energy, passion'.[2] Its reputation as a foundation stone of Italian Romantic opera lay in both its choice of Gothic subject (based on Charles Maturin's play *Bertram*) and its greater emphasis on a judicious use of *'canto declamato'* – a declamatory, syllabic setting of text.

Following the favourable reception of *Il pirata*, Bellini turned his energies towards revising his earlier work, *Bianca e Gernando* (Teatro di San Carlo, Naples, 1826) for a new production (as *Bianca e Fernando*) in Genoa in 1828. And then came a second contract for La Scala for the spring of 1829.[3] Initially, Bellini feared that the juxtaposition of a revival of *Il pirata* and an entirely new opera of unknown merit in the same season might damage his reputation with Milanese audiences.[4] Yet *La straniera* (14th February 1829) proved to be even more successful than *Il pirata*, garnering plaudits for its experimental use of arioso and *canto declamato*, which gave parts of the score an almost conversational feel in comparison to the heavily ornamented lines of Rossinian style – while also attracting criticism for not adhering sufficiently to Italian traditions of song.[5]

Bellini's next commissions came from Parma (*Zaira*, 16th May 1829) and Venice (*I Capuleti e i Montecchi*, 11th March 1830). And then in the summer of 1830 he signed contracts for three

---

2   *Gazzetta privilegiata di Milano,* 5th November 1827, see Francesco Pastura, *Bellini secondo la storia* (Parma: Guanda, 1959), p. 119.

3   Pastura, op. cit., pp. 140–41.

4   Ibid., pp. 142–43.

5   *Il censore universale*, 18th February 1829, I/14, p. 54.

new operas: the last works he would ever compose for Italian theatres. The first was for the Teatro Carcano, an opera house on the edge of Milan's city centre that had recently become a serious rival to the state-sponsored La Scala; the second was for La Scala itself; and the third was for the Teatro La Fenice in Venice.

The librettist for all these operas (including the revised *Bianca e Gernando*) since the composer had arrived in Milan was Felice Romani. Some thirteen years older than Bellini, Romani was one of the most respected and experienced librettists of his generation. Across an operatic career lasting just over two decades (1813–34), he produced ninety libretti for forty different composers, including Johann Simon Mayr, Saverio Mercadante, Gioachino Rossini, Stefano Pavesi, Nicola Vaccai, Giovanni Pacini, Gaetano Donizetti and Giacomo Meyerbeer. Many of those libretti were set a number of times (for example, *Francesca da Rimini* attracted the efforts of eleven different composers in total), and so Romani's impact on the operatic marketplace of his day was considerable. His hallmark, according to one of Bellini's more recent biographers, John Rosselli, was a clarity of expression that paved a route out of the more florid elements of Rossinian style towards the simpler, more direct approaches of mid-nineteenth-century Italian opera.[6] Bellini commented on precisely that quality on 1st July 1835: 'Romani's fine diction, clear, and yet not commonplace, vibrates and touches the heart!'[7] Bellini used Romani as his librettist for seven of his ten operas, and by the time of *Norma* they had already worked together on five operas. The relationship between the two men up to that point was largely cordial, although both experienced some exasperation on occasion – Bellini mainly on account of Romani's frequent tardiness with supplying the libretto, Romani because at times he was required by Bellini to set words to pre-composed melodies.

---

6 John Rosselli, *The Life of Bellini* (Cambridge: Cambridge University Press, 1996), p. 42.
7 Bellini to Paul Barroilhet, 1st July 1835; Luisa Cambi, *Vincenzo Bellini: Epistolario* (Verona: Mondadori, 1943), p. 571.

Giuditta Pasta

Central to Bellini's forthcoming three Italian contracts would be the soprano Giuditta Pasta (1797–1865). Her career had begun modestly enough in a small theatre in Milan in 1816. Unusually, she then immediately found employment at the Théâtre-Italien in Paris (through the patronage of composer Ferdinando Paer), followed by a stint at the King's Theatre in London. Pasta then returned to Italy, heavily pregnant with a daughter who was born in 1818. Re-emerging from that short absence from the stage with a more fully developed and controlled voice and with increasingly expressive gifts, she swiftly began to command attention. By the mid-1820s, she was assuredly the singer of the decade, enshrined in Stendhal's lavish plaudits in his biography of Rossini published in 1824. Many notes of Pasta's 'remarkably rich voice', Stendhal wrote, were 'not only extremely fine in themselves, but have the ability to produce a kind of resonant and magnetic vibration, which, through some still unexplained combination of physical phenomena, exercises an instantaneous and hypnotic effect on the soul of the spectator':[8] it was 'a voice that can weave a spell of magic about the plainest word in the plainest recitative'.[9] Stendhal's suggestion that Pasta's voice hypnotized her listeners recalls ancient ideas of the siren, but framed now rather more within the vocabulary of science (as befitted the new industrial age) than that of mythology.

If for some listeners Pasta's voice held an irresistible allure, for others it was an uneven, husky sound, with the registers imperfectly balanced and joined together by a veiled middle section. Her skill lay in how she used this often recalcitrant instrument in the service of both music and drama – and how, in effect, she sang with her whole body, transmuting feeling into a marvellous interplay of gesture. In terms of repertory, her interests drew her to roles in which she could explore a range of theatrical effect.

---

8   Stendhal, *The Life of Rossini* (1824), trans. Richard N. Coe (London: John Calder, 1956), p. 374.

9   Ibid., p. 371.

The English critic Henry Fothergill Chorley described how she abandoned the part of Desdemona in Rossini's *Otello* in favour of the title role (in a version made for mezzo-soprano), producing an 'impression of something fierce, masterful, Oriental, the like of which had hardly, till she came, had been expressed in music'.[10] Indeed, Chorley claimed, it was by immersing herself fully in the drama that Pasta resolved her technical vocal problems: 'the defects of intonation to which she was liable either disappeared, or were forgotten in the consummate union of vocal art with human emotion'.[11] In modern parlance, Pasta would be described as a dramatic or *spinto* soprano, but her repertory encompassed both soprano and contralto roles and the critics of the day often referred to her as a mezzo-soprano.[12]

Much of Pasta's career from 1822 took place in Paris and London, with the exception of appearances at the Teatro di San Carlo in Naples during the winter season of 1826–27. Her triumphal re-entry into Milan was not until the 1829–30 season at the Teatro Carcano, where, to rapturous audiences, she sang some of her best-known roles: most notably in Rossini's *Semiramide*, *Tancredi* and *Otello*, Mayr's *Medea in Corinto* and Zingarelli's *Giulietta e Romeo*. Promptly dubbed the *diva del mondo* by the critic Carlo Ritorni, Pasta was offered another contract for the succeeding year, with the added attraction of two operas written expressly for her by the most innovative composers of the day, Donizetti and Bellini. For Donizetti, she would create the title role of *Anna Bolena*; for Bellini, that of *La sonnambula*.

This latter opera, which opened on 6th March 1831, was therefore the first time that Bellini, Romani and Pasta had worked together, although their acquaintance had begun many years previously (indeed, Bellini considered Pasta's daughter Clelia, despite her extreme youth and the disparity in their ages, as a possible future wife). The integration of their

---

10 Henry Fothergill Chorley, *Thirty Years' Musical Recollections*, 2 vols. (London: Hurst & Blackett, 1862), Vol. I, p. 41.

11 Ibid.

12 See also Roger Parker's 'Note on Vocal Roles' at the end of his article in this guide, p. 41 [Ed.].

talents in *La sonnambula*, a *semi-seria* opera that combined a pastoral setting with the acrobatic feat of sleepwalking across a rickety bridge above a mill wheel, immediately won over the audience. Partnering Pasta, who played the eponymous heroine, was the tenor Giambattista Rubini. The Russian composer Mikhail Glinka was in the audience for one performance, and remarked that the singers did all they could to support 'their beloved maestro': 'They were singing and acting with such inner conviction as to weep real tears in the second act, drawing the public also into their emotion.' Everyone wept, wrote Glinka, including himself.[13]

Soumet's Norma

Pasta had already been contracted as *prima donna assoluta* for the 1831–32 season at La Scala: her first appearance at that theatre. It was imperative, therefore, to find a subject for the new opera in a very different vein from the rural idyll of *La sonnambula*. The choice eventually fell on a play recently staged in Paris at the Théâtre de l'Odéon: Alexandre Soumet's *Norma, ou L'infanticide*. It had opened on 6th April 1831, with the renowned Marguerite George (1787–1867) in the title role.[14]

Situated in the Faubourg Saint-Germain, the Théâtre de l'Odéon had been licensed as one of four main theatres in Paris in 1806, along with the Comédie-Française, the Opéra-Comique and the Opéra.[15] The Odéon was the first Parisian theatre to install gas lighting in 1820, and became known in succeeding years for its championship of the new school of French Romanticism, particularly under the directorship of Charles-Jean Harel from 1829 to 1831. Harel also brought back to the Odéon Mlle George, who had first appeared there in 1821 – and with whom Harel had maintained a long-standing (if not always exclusive) amorous partnership since 1818. George's reputation rested on her talents as both celebrated actress and *demi-mondaine*

13 Giorgio Appolonia, *Giuditta Pasta: Gloria del bel canto* (Turin: EDA, 2000), p. 144.

14 There is much confusion about the date of this premiere, which is variously given as 16th or 26th April. The date on Soumet's printed drama is 6th April 1831.

15 Albert W. Halsall, *Victor Hugo and the Romantic Drama* (Toronto: University of Toronto Press, 1998), p. 21.

through her affair with Napoleon Bonaparte (among others). She created a number of strong female roles for Soumet, including the eponymous heroines of *Jeanne d'Arc* and *Cléopâtre* (both 1824); for Victor Hugo, she would create the title roles of *Lucrèce Borgia* (1833) and *Marie Tudor* (1833); her repertory also included Lady Macbeth and Semiramis (in the play by Voltaire). A description of George in 1839 demonstrates the grandeur of her style:

> Mlle Georges [sic] seems to belong to a prodigious and lost race; she astonishes as much as she charms us. One might call her a woman of Titan, a Cybele, mother of gods and men, with her crenellated crown: her build that has something of Cyclops and the Pelasgians. Seeing her, one feels that she remains upright, like a granite column, in order to serve as a witness to an annihilated generation, and that she is the last representative of an epic and superhuman type. She is an admirable statue to place on the tomb of tragedy, now buried for all time. [16]

Soumet's five-act drama of *Norma*, with its echoes of Chateaubriand's *Les Martyrs* and Euripides' *Medea*, drew substantially on these attributes of Mlle George, and caused something of a stir when first performed. Summarizing his *flâneur*'s stroll among the Parisian theatres that season, Louis Véron remarked:

> Then finally you cross the bridges, you sink into the solitude of the Saint-Germain district; far away, very far, as in a fairy tale, you see a glimmer begin to appear that ends by becoming a dazzling light, it is the gas of the Odéon, it is Norma, grandiloquent and alexandrine success, Norma the infanticide and the druidess, Norma of M. Soumet, Norma of Mlle Georges [sic], Norma who weeps, who threatens, who terrifies, who slashes... [17]

---

16 The author was probably Théophile Gautier in *Les Belles Femmes de Paris par des hommes de lettres et des hommes du monde* (Paris: n.p., 1839), pp. 51–4.

17 Louis Désiré Véron, 'Revue dramatique', *Revue de Paris*, Vol. 26 (Bureau de la Revue de Paris, 1831), pp. 132–33.

From play to libretto: Norma re-envisaged

The circumstances surrounding the choice of *Norma* as the subject of Bellini's new opera remain uncertain. The play first appeared in Paris in early April; by 20th July Romani had apparently already finished the initial outline of the libretto. Neither Romani nor Bellini can be accurately placed in Paris during those intervening months; Pasta was singing in Milan up until 27th March, and then in London from 12th May to 28th July. However, mention was made of Soumet's play in the Italian cultural journal, *L'Eco* on 24th June 1831:

PARIS. The repertory of the Parisian theatres offers at the moment a vast field for singular reflection. While the law seems to abhor the spectacle of the guilty under the executioner's axe, at the Comédie-Française every evening is staged *Camille Desmoulins and his friends at the guillotine* [Blanchard and Magnan's *Camille Desmoulins, ou les Partis en 1794*]. At the Odéon, one watches *Norma kill her own children*. At the Gaieté, the *Marchese di Fabras* is strangled [Merville and Sauvage's *Favras*, also set at the time of the French Revolution]. At the Porte-Saint-Martin, *Antony stabs his lover* [Dumas's *Antony*]. At the Opéra, *Masaniello* [Auber's *La muette de Portici*] is shot dead, and at a theatre on the boulevards, *Ugolino* feasts on human flesh [Millevoye's *Ugolin*].[18]

Romani had already drawn substantially on classical and more recent French sources (Corneille, Voltaire, Pixérécourt, Hugo and Ducange) for his libretti, and he undoubtedly kept an eye out for interesting new work from the Parisian theatres. Although it is unlikely that the item above was the source of his information about Soumet's play, it is worth noting that for a librettist in search of a play with a strong central role for a prima donna, *Norma* is the only one in that summary that would fit the bill. The subject matter would also have appealed to Romani, who had supplied the libretto for an earlier opera on the same historical period, *La sacerdotessa d'Irminsul* (Pacini, 1820), as well as collaborating with Antonio Peracchi on a

18 *L'Eco*, 24th June 1831, IV/75, p. 300. Italics as in the original [Ed.].

six-volume dictionary of mythology and antiquity published between 1809 and 1825.

Little is known of the actual process of composition. Bellini makes only sparse references to the work in his extant letters. An early exchange emerged between Bellini and the tenor Domenico Donzelli, already also contracted by La Scala. On 3rd May, Donzelli, aware that Bellini was about to compose a new work for the opening of the season, provided the composer with valuable information about his vocal abilities:

> The range, then, of my voice is almost two octaves from low D to high C, singing in chest voice up until G; and it is in this range that I can declaim with equal vigour and sustain the full strength of declamation. From G to high C I can use falsetto, which employed with art and strength can be used as an ornament. I have sufficient agility, but descending rather than ascending passages are much easier by far for me.[19]

Bellini replied on 7th June that he would do his best to compose an opera suited to Donzelli's talents:

> The mainstays of my composition are only Donzelli and La Pasta; therefore the plot of the opera must revolve around these two artists, while the others will appear as stars directed by these two suns.[20]

The first indication that the subject of the work had been determined is a letter from Romani to La Scala's impresario Giuseppe Crivelli on 20th July 1831. Here, however, *Norma* is not mentioned directly: we learn only that that Romani had just heard from Bellini that matters had been agreed with Giulietta Grisi (who would sing Adalgisa), and that he should therefore set to work on the libretto 'of which I have already made the outline'.[21] Three days later Bellini himself wrote

---

19 Pastura, op. cit., p. 287.
20 Bellini to Donzelli, 7th June 1831; ibid., p. 288.
21 Alessandro Roccatagliati, *Felice Romani librettista* (Lucca: Libreria Musicale Italiana, 1996), p. 100.

from Como to his friend Alessandro Lamperi: 'I have already chosen
the subject for my new opera and it is a tragedy by Soumet entitled
Norma, ossia L'infanticidio, currently performed at Paris with great
success.'[22] The next mention of the opera occurs in a brief letter to
Bellini's mistress, Giuditta Turina, on 31st August: 'Romani told me
yesterday that he had completed a couple of numbers and will let
me read them this morning; if they please me perhaps tomorrow
I will begin to compose.'[23] And the following day Bellini wrote to
Pasta, then in Paris:

> I must now apply myself to the opera of which Romani gave me the
> plot only yesterday. I hope this subject will be to your taste. Romani
> believes it to be highly effective, and ideal for your encyclopaedic
> character, because such is that of Norma. He will arrange things
> in such a way that the situations won't bear any resemblance to
> other subjects, and he will adjust and even change the characters
> if that should prove necessary to make more effect. You will have
> already read it; if some thoughts about it come to mind, write to
> me. Meanwhile, get hold of the costume designs for the characters
> as they are performed in Paris; and if you don't find them in good
> taste and believe you can improve them, then do so.[24]

Bellini's comment about the 'encyclopaedic' nature of Pasta referred
to her ability to present a rounded characterization. The role of
Amina in *La sonnambula*, Romani remarked on one occasion, might
at first sight appear easy, but in fact required the interplay of subtle
characteristics: the singer had to be 'pure, ingenuous, innocent' and
at the same time 'passionate, sensitive, loving'; she had to possess 'a
cry of joy as well as one of grief, an accent of reproof as well as one
of prayer'; her movements and sighs should demonstrate something
of both idealism and truth; her singing had to be 'simple yet ornamented, both spontaneous and yet controlled, both perfect and yet
not apparently studied'. This, concluded Romani, was what had been

---

22 Bellini to Lamperi, 23rd July 1831; Cambi, op. cit., p. 275.

23 Ibid., p. 278.

24 Ibid., p. 278–89.

created by Bellini's 'poetic intellect' and fully realized by Giuditta Pasta.[25] As we will see, this ability to project a multifaceted portrayal was something that the printed drama of Soumet's *Norma* suggested was shared by both Mlle George and Norma herself.

To another correspondent, Bellini confirmed that he was working on the opera ('I find it interesting, and if Romani extracts good poetry from it then a good libretto will emerge'),[26] but revealed that his concentration had been hampered by the threat of cholera creeping across Italy. Yet by 7th September he could tell Giuditta Turina that 'I have almost finished the overture of the opera and sketched out a chorus for the Introduzione, and I am not unhappy with them'.[27] In the meantime, Bellini was also engaged with other aspects of his business as a composer, considering questions of copyright concerning his earlier operas, and discussing a possible forthcoming contract with the Teatro di San Carlo in Naples. It is from correspondence regarding that contract that we learn in a letter of 19th September that his fee for *Norma* at La Scala was 12,000 Austrian lire: an exceptionally large sum for the period.[28] Of the rehearsals that began in early December there remains only a brief, undated note to the music publisher Giovanni Ricordi's secretary, Giovanni Cerri, regarding some corrections in the chorus 'Guerra, guerra!'[29]

While Bellini's correspondence therefore provides only limited information about the progress of the opera's composition, the sketches of various numbers offer some insights. From these, explored initially by Franco Schlitzer, it is apparent that had Bellini set Romani's original version the work would have been much longer. Some alterations, such as those to the text of 'Casta Diva', were made partly in response to the censor's anxieties about overt martial allusions. It is also apparent that the requirements of the singers necessitated certain changes: the realization that the bass Vincenzo Negrini (Oroveso) was suffering from a heart condition, for example, meant that his original solo in

---

25 Emilia Branca, *Felice Romani* (Turin, Florence and Rome: Ermanno Loescher, 1882), p. 165.

26 Cambi, op. cit., p. 280.

27 Bellini to Giuditta Turina, 7th September 1831; ibid., p. 281.

28 Ibid., p. 283.

29 Ibid., p. 289.

Act Two had to be distributed elsewhere in the opera, leading to its interpolation in the opening chorus. And Bellini's lack of confidence (expressed in various letters after the first performance) about the duet between Pollione and Adalgisa is borne out by the numerous different drafts made in that section of the score.

Adapting Soumet's drama to the operatic stage required considerable changes, beginning with the reduction of its five acts to a two-act structure. The cast is pared down to concentrate primarily on Norma (confining her two sons to non-speaking roles), Pollione, Adalgisa and Oroveso. One important change is in the narrative's relationship to ideas of Christianity. In the play, Clotilde (Norma's confidante) is a Christian convert; in Act Three she discusses her vision of God with Agénor, Norma's elder son, leading him to declare after Clotilde's departure, 'Pourquoi ma mère, hélas! n'est-elle pas chrétienne? / J'aurais besoin d'un dieu qui rassure et soutienne' ['Why, alas, is my mother not a Christian? I have need of a god who reassures and supports me'] (Act Three, Scene One). The opera instead sets the pagan world of the Druids against the martial empire of the Romans without this additional religious framing. Yet there are more subtle Christian inflections in the opera. In the drama, Pollion makes various accusations of barbarity against the Gauls: the ultimate blood-soaked actions of Norma as well as Orovèse's intransigence both seem to bear out his perspective. In contrast, the opera in its emphasis on self-sacrifice and reconciliation reveals a society in the process of learning and thus adheres more closely to classical notions of the purpose of tragedy (exemplified by the ancient Greeks and Shakespeare) rather than as nihilistic slaughter in post-French Revolution Romantic terms. While arguably less 'modern' than its dramatic source, by tapping into the template of older narrative structures the opera perhaps secured a more lasting future.

The most striking difference is in the excision of the play's final act, which begins with Adalgise returning from the Roman camp to reveal that Pollion now wishes to atone by marrying Norma; Orovèse (Norma's father) refuses the proposal, proclaiming that 'La mort pour le coupable est un don précieux' ['For the guilty, death is a precious gift']. Left alone, Adalgise is found by Agénor, alarmed by his mother's frightening state of mind. Norma herself appears, clearly deranged and making ominous references to the sleep of her younger son Clodomir. Then Pollion arrives and declares that he still loves Norma. This admission does little to release Norma from her madness: she remains locked in delirious thoughts of guilt and death. The source of these dark images is finally revealed when the murdered body of Clodomir is discovered in a nearby cave. Now the memory of that deed is terrifyingly restored to Norma, and she drags Agénor into the rocks. Orovèse arrives to witness Pollion emerging from the cave with the body of Clodomir; all then see, on the far side of the lake, Agénor struggling with his mother. He faints; Norma makes a last pronouncement:

> Aux bords de ces abîmes
> Viens, viens d'un seul regard embrasser tous tes crimes,
> Et de nos corps sanglants recherchant les lambeaux,
> Épouser Adalgise, entre nos trois tombeaux.[30]

And then, clutching Agénor, she leaps. Pollion cries 'Ah! Je meurs!' ['Ah! I die!]. Orovèse responds: 'Tu vivras en proie à sa démence. / Son supplice finit; Romain, le tien commence' ['You will live in the grip of her madness. / Her suffering ends; yours, Roman, begins'].

The impact of this scene in Paris is alluded to in a curious footnote in the printed drama at the beginning of Norma's mad scene in the final act, when she realizes that she has killed her son Clodomir:

Mademoiselle George attained sublime heights here; after having been in turn during the first four acts of *Norma* the ancient Greeks' Niobe and Medea, Shakespeare's Lady Macbeth and Châteaubriand's Vélléda; after having travelled the entire circle of passions enclosed in a woman's heart, it was astonishing that she yet found such harrowing and pathetic levels; and one needed to

---

30 'On the brink of this abyss / Come, come, embrace all your crimes with a single glance, / And retrieving the fragments of our bloodied bodies, / Marry Adalgisa, among our three tombs.'

have seen her deliver these mad scenes in order to understand the full power of her tragic inspiration, rendered still more striking by contrast with the young Tom, who played the role of Agénor with admirable grace and sweetness.[31]

This footnote (presumably by Soumet himself) is almost certainly the main source of Bellini's comment about the 'encyclopaedic character' of Norma.

The decision to exclude this mad scene substantially altered the opera's narrative. It almost certainly owed something to Bellini's assurance to Pasta that any resemblance to earlier subjects would be avoided. Certainly, as the drama stands it bears more than a little similarity to Medea's vengeful act of infanticide, as was noted by the French critics. Medea was a role (in Mayr's *Medea in Corinto*) in which Pasta had already excelled in the 1820s; she had also exhibited her skill in mad scenes in the two operas most recently written for her in 1831 during her Milanese sojourn, Donizetti's *Anna Bolena* and Bellini's own *La sonnambula*. For Milan's audience especially, then, yet another mad scene was surely out of the question.

The excision of Soumet's final act allows the opera to pursue the logic of Norma's attempt to protect Adalgisa more fully: in the play, it is odd that this generous action is then followed by her slaughter of her sons. The operatic Norma gains in nobility by remaining in full possession of her mental faculties, and in ensuring in her fervent debate with Oroveso the protection of her children after her death.

Bellini and Romani composed the role of Norma in a way that gave full scope to Pasta's vocal abilities, and which made virtues out of her perceived inadequacies. Markings in the score such as *con voce soffocata* or *con voce repressa* indicated where her veiled tone could be used to imposing dramatic effect. So too were the gestural possibilities of the role given careful treatment, as in the scene in Act Two where Norma considers – but ultimately decides against – the murder of her children. Bellini not only crafted his music to display Pasta's existing talents, he also foresaw her potential. Pasta reportedly

---

31 Alexandre Soumet, *Norma. Tragédie en cinq actes et en* vers (Paris: J. N. Barba, 1831), p. 84.

considered 'Casta Diva', the prayer to the moon goddess, as initially beyond her capabilities, and was only persuaded by Bellini to attempt it with reluctance and when it had been transposed a tone lower to F major. And yet it was one of the best-received numbers in the early performances, as the critic of the Milanese journal *Corriere delle dame* recorded on 30th December 1831: 'its magical notes are so sweetly and so magisterially performed by Pasta that it is a marvel if the invoked goddess does not descend to gladden both singer and maestro with her celestial image'.[32] On the day of the premiere, Pasta had sent Bellini a gift of an embroidered lampshade and a posy of silk flowers ('this lamp by night and these flowers by day were witnesses to my studies for *Norma*') to thank him for his patience in enabling her to transcend 'the immense fear that persecuted me when I found myself little suited to performing your sublime harmonies'.[33] Bellini thus not only responded in compositional terms to Pasta's vocal attributes, but extended them by writing new challenges. There is a certain irony in the fact that Pasta's voice, so often criticized for its technical failings, produced a role which soon came to be seen as the apotheosis of technical perfection. Norma – and 'Casta Diva' in particular – became the means by which many a later soprano tested her levels of vocal accomplishment.

The Premiere

Did Bellini await the evening of the premiere with some trepidation? Or had the reception of his other three operas for Milan lulled him into confident anticipation of a similarly enthusiastic reaction? Inexplicably, to his mind, the response to that first night of *Norma* was muted. Bellini was angry and puzzled: if we are to believe a much disputed letter published by Florimo, he regarded the opera as a 'worthy sister' to his earlier Milanese compositions and could not understand why the audience did not see likewise.[34] He attributed blame for the audience's response to the machinations of

32   *Il corriere delle dame*, 30th December 1831, 72, pp. 570–71.

33   Pastura, op. cit., p. 295.

34   Cambi, op. cit., pp. 291–93 and 296–97.

Giulia Samoyloff, the mistress of a rival composer, Giovanni Pacini, as well as hostility to Pasta among certain figures at La Scala. The journals, however, pointed to the nature of Bellini's music, with its defiance of convention in operatic structure (such as the absence of a concertato finale to the first act) and declamatory emphasis. Whatever the reason, the audience's initially tepid response nonetheless grew ever warmer during the succeeding performances; by the end of December Bellini could write in more confident terms about the opera's success. It had thirty-four performances at La Scala that season, before being taken up in other theatres in Italy and abroad. Its longevity has assured it a reputation as the greatest example of Bellini and Romani's collaboration, and as the fullest imprint of the majestic talents of Giuditta Pasta.

Yet there is a postscript to that triumph. With two extraordinary achievements (*La sonnambula* and *Norma*) behind them, Bellini, Romani and Pasta might have faced their next contract together, at La Fenice in 1833, with some equanimity. And yet *Beatrice di Tenda*, which was to be their last collaboration, decisively fractured the relationship between the two men, and was received poorly. It remains a signal illustration of the fleeting, elusive nature of theatrical success.

Norma's Musical Journey

Roger Parker

Vincenzo Bellini's *Norma* bears traces of its immediate operatic climate (in particular a debt to Rossinian forms that was shared by all his contemporaries), but what is continually surprising is the extent to which the composer managed to defy or ignore or enrich formal expectations. There is a sense in which, even from his very first student work, *Adelson e Salvini* (1825), we can hear this tendency to avoid the currently fashionable, in particular to prefer the sentimental simplicity of Neapolitan-school composers of a generation earlier (notably Giovanni Paisiello and Domenico Cimarosa) rather than slavishly follow what has become known as the 'code Rossini', with its succession of multi-movement set pieces for arias, duets and larger ensembles. What is more, by the time of *Norma* we know from Bellini's letters that he was also making a conscious effort to be 'original': he separated himself from the common run and – as is so well known – in the process became an object of veneration for future composers, some of them otherwise dismissive of the entire bel canto tradition. To chart all this is beyond the scope of this article, but I have taken the liberty, in the course of my journey through the opera, to linger (and lingering is, after all, a very Bellinian gesture) on a couple of moments ('Casta Diva' in Act One and 'In mia man' in Act Two) that seem to me to represent the musical heart of the work. It should go without saying that the rest deserves similar attention.

Sinfonia

Bellini's great opera begins on a suitably grand scale, declaring its classical grandeur by offering the spectator a formal Sinfonia (Overture) rather than the shorter, atmospheric preludes more usual in Romantic *melodramma*. Sometimes such overtures are little more than pot-pourri confections. The one that introduces Donizetti's *Anna Bolena* is a good case in point: written at huge speed at the very last minute, in part it cobbles together, none too subtly, some melodies from the opera. There are elements of that technique here, but – as we might expect – Bellini wanted something more elaborate and, above all, something more intricately worked. An altogether un-Donizettian fussiness is evident right at the start, in which the opening, minor-mode, full-orchestral gestures are written in a complex rhythmic pattern that ensures a particular weight to each chord [1].[1] This call to arms is then interrupted by two bars, Lento, for solo flute and clarinet, then by a near-quotation from the jaunty dotted rhythms that will introduce the opera's heroine and then by an agitated string melody, full of 'sighing' figures and anxious semiquavers. What one might call a second subject finally appears (in the tonic major [2]), this time an obvious quotation from the Act Two duet between Norma and Pollione. From that point the overture takes the material through what we might call some 'developmental', symphonic moves; the duet melody turns up in a near-related key and we might seem to be heading for a stormy close back in the home minor. But instead something extraordinary happens. The texture changes: in a sudden move to major, tremolo lower strings, trilling first violins, sustained wind chords and harp arpeggios describe a meandering chord progression in a passage resembling the sublime, soaring music at the end of the Act Four finale of Rossini's *Guillaume Tell*.[2] Then the stormy music returns to round off the movement.

---

1   Numbers in square brackets refer to the Thematic Guide on pp. 70–73 [Ed.].
2   *Guillaume Tell* had its premiere at the Théâtre de L'Académie Royale de Musique in Paris in August 1829. Its first performances in Italy, at the Teatro di San Carlo, Naples, were not until 1833. There is no reliable documentation of Bellini having been familiar with the score, but the similarity between the two passages is striking [Ed.].

What does it all *mean*? Certainly there are hints that this is the drama *in nuce*: passion and unrest vie with elegant, Italianate melody; but that almost static, almost *ecstatic* music near the close? Outdoor music? A hint of the unpredictable, sublime nature of the heroine? It's an enigma which won't entirely be solved in the drama that follows.

Act One

1. Introduzione

An Introduzione was, by this stage in nineteenth-century Italian opera, a well-known entity. It had a scene-setting function, sonically embodied by the chorus, around which could be wrapped a standard two-movement entrance aria for one of the lesser principals. In one sense, the present Introduzione does just that; but it does so in a way that fashions something entirely different. The scene directions are vital:

> The Druids' holy forest. In the middle is the oak of Irminsul and at the foot of it is the Druids' altar stone. In the distance are wood-covered hills. It is night, and distant fires can be made out in the woods.

It is, then, a mysterious, ancient, nocturnal ambience, something that the evocative orchestral introduction immediately conjures up. In the same key and open mood of the 'Maggiore' section in the Sinfonia, *divisi* violas and cellos sound forth what is clearly a processional theme, akin (although though it's unlikely Bellini would have known it) to the priests' solemn march in Mozart's *Die Zauberflöte*. The music increases in grandeur as the Druids mass on stage, and then the entire sequence is repeated over the opening melody assigned to Oreveso, head of the Druids and Norma's father ('Ite sul colle, o Druidi' ['O Druids, go up on to the hill'] [3]). Oroveso's opening address also builds in intensity, in particular as the Druids anxiously wonder whether Norma will appear. An affirmative from Oroveso unleashes a cabaletta that seems to look forward to early Verdi, full of martial dotted rhythms and expansive arpeggios ('Dell'aura tua profetica / terribil Dio, l'informa' ['Fearful god, imbue her / with your spirit of prophecy'] [4]); and Verdian too is the fact that the male chorus of Druids plays a prominent melodic role, even to the extent of leading off the entire section in choral unison. Oroveso joins in and the music moves to the usual triumphant cadences; but then, entirely against expectations, a return to the processional of the scene's opening accompanies the Druids as they disperse into the forest, only scattered string triplets giving a hint of the energy that had previously been unleashed. And that return to the solemn ambience of the opening is crucial: we have indeed been introduced to one of the opera's principal singers via the usual two-movement aria; but – far more important – we have experienced an introduction to *Norma*'s particular world, that strange mixture of the warlike and mistily Romantic that is so vital a part of its overall articulation.

2. Recitativo e Cavatina Pollione

As perhaps suits the character, and the star soloist who was cast in the part, this multi-movement entrance aria for Pollione, the Roman proconsul in Gaul, is much more conventional than was Oroveso's: it follows more obviously the standard format of recitative, slow move- ment, *tempo di mezzo* (that is, a linking section) and closing cabaletta. Within that format, though, there are plenty of surprises. An agitated string introduction, perhaps betraying something of Pollione's nerv- ousness at being caught between two women, Norma and Adalgisa, introduces an extended recitative with his companion Flavio. Bellini's recitative elsewhere in the opera, particularly for his heroine, can be enormously intricate; but here (and doubtless in consideration of the elaborate background plot details that need to be unfolded) it is disarmingly simple, recalling the old continuo-accompanied recita- tive of the earlier Neapolitan school in which the composer learned his trade. The slow moment, when Pollione tells Flavio his dream of being in Rome with Adalgisa ('Meco all'altar di Venere / era Adalgisa in Roma' ['Adalgisa was beside me / at the altar of Venus in Rome'] [5]), then allows the singer to display his range, with Bellini making sure that his star tenor, Domenico Donzelli, could enjoy a melody that fitted his robust voice and also had an opportunity to display his high C – a note he would have taken in falsetto but nevertheless with some considerable force. This movement is in the form of a narrative and thus, as tradition dictated, in two stanzas. It starts off conventionally, both melodically and in accompaniment, as Pollione recalls his dream. But then, as he describes the 'terribile... ombra' ('dreadful shadow') that suddenly descended, the mood darkens and a restless motif in the bass takes over, one whose presence then seems to infect the rest of the narrative. The *tempo di mezzo* is heralded by distant trumpet fanfares and a *banda* statement of the Druids' signature march theme, and this mood seems to influence Pollione, whose cabaletta ('Me protegge, me difende / un poter maggior di loro' ['A power greater than theirs / protects and defends me'] [6]) is very similar in tone: again there are those jaunty dotted rhythms and energetic rising arpeggios. Is there a sense of anxiousness also here, a sense that Pollione tries too hard to banish that dreadful shadow which the Druids have cast over him (in his dream)? One could argue thus, but Italian opera of this period is in some ways resistant to such psychological complexities; it is more likely that Bellini's command of this extrovert idiom was relatively undifferentiated, and had to serve for both the Druids and their chief antagonist.

3. Coro, Scena e Cavatina Norma

As so often in Italian opera, *Norma* starts with a 'portrait gallery' approach to narrative exposition, one where the plot unfolds via a sequence of solo scenes in which characters are each given multi-movement arias. And, again traditionally, there is in *Norma* a distinct sense of hierarchy in the build-up, with each scene weightier than the last as the characters increase in importance. All this is to say that the moment we hear the grand, hymn-like full-orchestral introduction to this, Norma's solo scene [7], there can be no doubt that she is indeed intended to be the major focus of our attention in the drama. What emerges, though, is entirely unprecedented in Italian opera of the period. The Druids' march re-appears in what might be called its definitive version [8], but this time serves to introduce and then punctuate the chorus, who welcome Norma with religious solemnity. As Norma appears, 'surrounded by her ministers', she launches into a recitative very different from that in the previous scene. Here there is a variation of utterance that compellingly belongs to the heroine: underpinned by a constantly changing orchestral texture, seemingly attentive to her every utterance, she takes us through a gamut of emotions, first angrily quelling her warlike followers, then assuring them that she will eventually prevail over the hated oppressors, and finally leading the mood into one of calm worship.

The aria that follows, 'Casta Diva', in which Norma invokes the goddess of the moon, is justly one of the most famous in the bel canto repertory, a piece endlessly recycled in arrangements during the nineteenth century. We can imagine from it something of the unique abilities of the first Norma, Giuditta Pasta, and the adulation she could excite, as well as the particular alchemy at work between her voice and the composer's musical invention. Although Bellini initially made his mark, in operas such as *La straniera* and *Il pirata*, by differentiating his melodic style from that of Rossini, by the time of *Norma* he could again deploy Rossinian vocal gestures; however, he would use such gestures sparingly, forever interrupting the line with the expressive, declamatory lingering and pauses that had become his trademark.

The opening of 'Casta Diva' is a demonstration of the best that Bellini could achieve in this vein [9]. It has often been celebrated as a classic, but the peculiar qualities of the aria, its sense of slow development over two long verses, are dictated by the dramatic situation, as a priestly incantation. Romani's words are set in telling poetic shapes, but they are also simple and direct:

> Casta Diva, che inargenti
> queste sacre antiche piante,
> a noi volgi il bel sembiante,
> senza nube e senza vel! [3]

Bellini freely repeats individual words and phrases, but this repetition is far from mechanical, not merely employed to fill out the musical phrases. If isolated from their music, the words would indeed be a

---

3 'Chaste goddess, who makes silver / these ancient sacred trees, / turn your beautiful face to us, / unveiled and unclouded!'

repetitious gabble: 'Casta Diva, casta Diva, che inargenti, queste sacre, queste sacre, queste sacre antiche piante'; but when attached to the musical phrases each of the verbal repetitions contributes to the intensity. The first syllables of 'Casta Diva' and 'queste sacre' are stretched out and then ornamented, so much so that the literal meaning of the words is obscured; but the urgent repetitions then make certain that the essential sentiment is communicated. In spite of the fragmentation – the momentary pauses that articulate each tiny musical phrase – this very long melody (one of the many such that Verdi so admired) progresses towards a remarkable climax on 'sembiante', one whose uppermost notes (A to B flat) repeat an octave higher the opening two notes of the entire melody.

After such a remarkable aria, the continuation of the scene is perhaps inevitably something of an anticlimax. The Druids' march returns yet again, and Norma establishes her regal authority by detonating a series of Rossinian vocal flourishes, but then she retreats into an interior world, the one in which she secretly loves Pollione, and thus precipitates her closing cabaletta, 'Ah! bello a me ritorna / del fido amor primiero' ('Ah, come back to me, charming, / as in the days of our first, devoted love') [10]. Again the adjective 'Rossinian' might be applied: this is an open-ended lyrical number, dissolving into ever more elaborate vocal exuberance as Norma remembers fondly her first, untroubled days with Pollione. But by the end, the Druids' march and the chorus again return; Norma's remembrances become ever more desperate, interrupting the brash world that surrounds her, until finally she and her followers retreat from the scene.

4. Duetto Adalgisa e Pollione

The orchestral introduction that ushers in Adalgisa, a young priestess at the temple of Irminsul, immediately characterizes her as someone very different from the outwardly imperious, inwardly passionate Norma. The repeated semiquaver motif speaks of hesitancy, albeit with a flute and clarinet melody that hints at her lyrical potential. Instead of an entrance aria (four in succession would be too many even for a bel canto portrait gallery) she has a passionate *arioso* begging for divine protection ('Deh! proteggimi, o Dio' ['Oh, protect me, o god']), an utterance that opens and closes with a beautiful orchestral peroration [11], prayerful and contemplative, showing Bellini's mastery of orchestration in its subtle blend of clarinets and strings. Pollione's entrance, deliberately jarring after this lyrical pause, introduces a formal multi-movement duet with more of Bellini's 'classical', unadorned recitative as Adalgisa rejects her former lover. As expected, there follows a so-called *tempo d'attacco*, underpinned by a driving string figure over which the warring couple exchange declamatory statements. Often such duets can have four movements, but here the *tempo d'attacco* moves immediately to a closing duet cabaletta ('Vieni in Roma' ['Come to Rome'] [12]) as Pollione pleads with Adalgisa to accompany him to Rome. This delicate melody is repeated by Adalgisa, and we might expect (as, for example, in *Lucia di Lammermoor*) a ensemble rendition, in octaves or parallel intervals, to close off the number. But Bellini offers something different and in many ways more compelling. He splits the melody irregularly between the two characters, making the melody become the basis of a *conversation* between them, one in which Pollione seems to use the sway of the music they have sung separately to cement his new conquest of Adalgisa. There could be no better illustration of the power that melodic expression seems to exert over the characters in this opera.

5. Scena e Terzetto finale

The action now moves to Norma's home, and the long scene that ensues is in two very different parts, divided by an abrupt change of mood. However, the flow of the number, its sense of musico-dramatic progression, is nevertheless undeniable. Open fifths in the woodwind and brass, perhaps reminiscent of the outdoor music of the overture and first scene, introduce a section of Bellinian Sturm und Drang, with agitated, minor-mode semiquaver motifs in the strings contrasted with an oboe melody characterized by sighing figures and breathless pauses. Norma, with her children as silent witnesses, laments in bare recitative to Clotilde, her confidante, over the dreadful conflict she feels between love for Pollione and love for the children they have had together. And then, in an oasis of calm, Adalgisa appears and confesses her own guilty secret. The first part of their duet again takes place in recitative, although with telling interjections of string chords to mark the sympathy between them; but then, as if through force of shared emotion, a lyrical movement emerges. The orchestral underpinning, which seems to feed and sustain their distracted reminiscences, is constructed with marvellous economy: pizzicato lower strings, rocking violin arpeggios, sustained violas as the emotional undercurrent and a high flute melody, as isolated as the two protagonists in the scene. Their exchange ('Oh! rimembranza!' ['Oh, memories!'] [13]) outwardly takes the form of a long melody first articulated by Norma and then, identically, by Adalgisa (the equality of their vocal ranges is obvious and necessary here, as in so many other parts of the score); but it is better described as another conversation through song, each of these wronged women interjecting sympathetic comments into the other's lament. This beautiful sequence leads directly to a closing cabaletta, 'Ah! sì, fa core' ('Ah, yes, take heart') [14], in which Norma agrees to release Adalgisa from her sacred vows and let her follow the dictates of her heart. It is a kind of celebration, both of private feelings over public duty, and of their sense of solidarity and shared concerns. The musical mode is, as perhaps befits a celebration, a triumphant return to the old Rossinian code in which Bellini had grown up, with a clear two-verse structure, elaborate fioritura and a closing section in which the two sopranos join in an elaborate cadenza in parallel thirds.

The second half of the scene brutally interrupts this sense of equilibrium, revealing as it does the central conflict that drives the entire drama. Pollione arrives, making it immediately obvious that Adalgisa's and Norma's anguished thoughts are directed towards the same object. In the bel canto tradition that had emerged from Rossinian usage, this halfway point and crux in the drama usually took the form of a so-called concertato finale, in which all the principals would come together with the chorus in a great scene of public confrontation and emotional release. But Bellini, in a move that some contemporary critics found disturbing, maintained the act-ending as an essentially private moment, providing an ensemble no bigger than a closing trio between the three principals. First comes the moment of revelation, with a return of agitated string semiquavers, then a huge outburst from Norma, one that in other formal circumstances would sound like a closing cabaletta of Rossinian vocal exuberance. This gives way to a remarkable terzetto ('Oh! di qual sei tu vittima' ['Oh, you are the victim'] [15]), marked Andante marcato and full of suppressed emotion, breathless attempts at melody over a spiky accompaniment. (In atmosphere and dramatic placement, if not in melodic contour, this trio seems the obvious inspiration for the final trio of Verdi's *Ernani* (1844), one of the younger composer's most radical experiments of his early years.) From there to the end of the act the tension never lets up, with desperate melodies following one after the other, culminating in the trio cabaletta 'Vanne, sì, mi lascia indegno' ['Yes, go; leave me you despicable man'] [16], marked 'assai agitato' and crowned at the end (perhaps a gesture to the concertato tradition) with an offstage chorus calling Norma to her religious duties.

Act Two

6. Scena e Duetto

One aspect of the closing number of Act One is the extent to which Norma begins to dominate the vocal and dramatic focus of the opera. In particular in the last part of the act, the terzetto finale, she leads off every single lyrical section, something highly unusual in a type of opera that generally attempted (and for obvious reasons) to divide the vocal spoils among two or even three *primi cantanti*. This focus is if anything intensified at the start of Act Two, which takes place inside Norma's home. While we might expect here a passionate solo for either Pollione or, especially, Adalgisa (who had no solo number in Act One), instead we are pitched again into Norma's interior world as she agonizes over the fate of her beloved children. Her opening recitative, preceded by an imposing string prelude with an 'antique' (that is, quasi-religious) part-writing and a lachrymose cello solo, is a magnificent demonstration of the faith the composer had in both the histrionic and lyrical qualities of his leading lady. All her powers of declamation, in some instances with minimal orchestral assistance, are needed in the opening passage ('Dormono entrambi' ['They are both asleep'] [17]), while her assumption of the cello melody ('Teneri figli' ['My dear children'] [18]) takes her high above the restrained orchestral accompaniment: as exposed vocally as she is psychologically.

Norma sends for Adalgisa, thus beginning what is in many ways the most conventional duet in the opera, at least from a formal point of view. It contains each of the four movements (*tempo d'attacco*, slow movement, *tempo di mezzo* and cabaletta) traditionally associated with such numbers on their grandest scale, which at first might seem odd, particularly because this is a duet that marks resolution and solidarity between its two characters. But perhaps that solidarity is precisely the point: this long duet is a still point of calm in a generally strife-torn opera, a necessary pause in intensity before the final tragedy begins.

After some typically spare recitative, the first moment (*tempo d'attacco*, 'Deh! con te li pendi' ['Please, take them with you'] [19]) might at first seem oddly sunny and untroubled: in a bright C major, with Bellini's trademark rocking strings, it presents patterned lyrical statements for Norma and Adalgisa, in both cases statements that dissolve into Rossinian vocal flourishes and a climax on high C (mezzo-soprano Adalgisas are often severely taxed, and the duet is frequently transposed a tone lower). This leads to the slow movement ('Mira, o Norma' ['Look, Norma'] [20]). Given the words (Adalgisa is pleading; Norma is resisting), one might expect a so-called 'dissimilar' movement here, but in fact the two are throughout locked in the same melodic embrace – a beautiful line that, typically for Bellini, is constantly punctuated by small pauses to increase its emotional edge and intensity. They begin the number with a patterned exchange of the melody, but soon they join in parallel thirds for a musical celebration of their closeness and mutual sympathy. After this lengthy indulgence, the final two movements must necessarily be speedier and less intricate. A typically disjunctive *tempo di mezzo*, driven by stock orchestral gestures, leads to the final cabaletta ('Sì, fino all'ore estreme / compagna tua m'avrai' ['Yes, you will have me as your friend / until your last hour'] [21]), which – as befits its sentiments – is in parallel thirds from the start and, in spite of being in the usual two strophes, seems in its brevity more like a coda to the duet than an independent movement.

7. Coro e Scena

The chorus in nineteenth-century Italian opera (at least before Verdi) can sometimes be a rather neutral force: ready when required to introduce a scene, swell a progress or lend vocal heft to the principals' sentiments, but hardly likely to become a force in its own right. This much might be said of the chorus in Act One of *Norma*, but in Act Two the Druid warriors take on for a time a distinct personality. Such a process begins here, as they are waiting, at times calmly, at times with explosive impatience, for the armed struggle to begin. 'Non partì?' ('Has he not left?') [22] has in many ways a trademark Bellinian sound: upper strings in arpeggios against sustained violas; a rich contingent of woodwind instruments, sometimes with martial dotted rhythms, but typically playing the parallel thirds so reminiscent of Italian folk music; and a choral melody, sometimes in the form of dialogue between the tenors and basses, both direct and intimate. Oroveso's subsequent number, 'Ah! del Tebro al giogo indegno / fremo io pure' ('I too rage at being / under the Roman yoke') [23], attempts to energize this rather lachrymose collective, but soon the idiom of 'Non partì' returns and all retreat into the hinterland from which they emerged.

8. Finale dell'Atto Secondo

The scene changes to the Temple of Irminsul, where this weighty finale will unfold in three sections. First comes a 'Scena e Coro'. In a rare moment of serenity, a brief continuation of the previous scene's calm-before-the-storm, Norma's brief scena again takes place in spare recitative, albeit with a final Rossinian outburst of coloratura. But then the spell is broken: Clotilde announces Adalgisa's failure to persuade Pollione to return to Norma and Norma summons the warlike chorus for their second significant outing in this act, the ferocious 'Guerra, guerra!' ('War, war!') [24]. In many ways this number is in vivid contrast to almost all the other music in the opera, with full orchestration that verges on the blatant, and with obsessively repeated melodic figures and rhythms, quite unlike Bellini's usual, flexible idiom. Small surprise, perhaps, that this number became a rallying cry for Italian patriots during the crises of 1848 and 1859, with tales of audiences joining in with the Druids that were repeated, with what accuracy we cannot judge, by a number of enthusiastic commentators.

The next section is a 'Scena e Duetto' between Norma and Pollione, and thus a confrontation that has been anticipated for the entire opera and constitutes its innermost core. It is ushered in, as befits such a moment, with some elaborately orchestrated recitative, plus a solemn orchestral march, replete with drum-roll 'death figures' as Pollione is led on. But then, where we might expect more violent confrontation, we witness a return to the more usual Bellinian manner, albeit with repressed overtones that are immediately obvious. The duet 'In mia man alfin tu sei' ('At last you are in my hands') [25] was famously commented upon by Verdi. Appended after his famous statement about the divine length of Bellini's melodies ('there are long, long melodies such as none before him had written') is a further comment: 'And what truth and power there is in his declamation – in the duet between Pollione and Norma, for instance'.[4] Rossini also praised the number, according to Bellini's lifelong friend Francesco Florimo, saying that 'The words are so enmeshed in the notes and the notes in the words that together they form a complete and perfect whole'.[5] Both realized that this is a prime example of the fact that Bellini had a great deal more than simply a melodic gift. He could, as so often in *Norma*, use melody to articulate dramatic situations. The start of 'In mia man alfin tu sei', which develops through numerous moods and movements, is the most remarkable. Like many lyrical sections, it is preceded by a leisurely instrumental introduction. The vocal line then unfolds in three statements of the main melody, an inspiration that – like so many of Bellini's greatest melodies – is made up of fragments that rise gradually to a melodic climax and then more

4   Stephen A. Willier, *Vincenzo Bellini: A Research and Information Guide* (New York and London: Routledge, 2nd edition 2009), p. 31.
5   Francesco Florimo, *La scuola musicale di Napoli e i suoi Conservatori*, Vol. III (Naples: Morano, 1880–84), p. 195.

swiftly descend to the initial register. In the first statement Norma establishes her dominance in a series of fragmentary utterances. The last of them, the four syllables of 'Io lo posso' ('I can do it'), is timed with the moment of melodic climax, and its detonation stimulates dialogue: the remainder of the melody is articulated through a hurried exchange between Norma and Pollione. The second statement is all Norma's, as she lays out her bargain, and now the four syllables of her rival's name, 'Adalgisa', are at the melodic climax, and their utterance seems to derail and extend the melody, which spins off into motivic and verbal repetitions. More rapid dialogue ensues, and the melody, whose shapes have so far controlled their exchange, is broken; modulations and new melodic ideas crowd in; indeed it becomes impossible to parse the duet in the traditional multi-movement forms we have identified earlier in the opera. Eventually, however, the music settles into a vehement cabaletta-coda, one in which the melody already heard in the overture features prominently.

The last section of *Norma* is a 'Scena ed Aria Finale', one of which the composer was justifiably proud, calling the passage 'A concertato and a stretta, both of them so original in style as to reduce to silence any enemies I might have'.[6] As might be expected, Norma's admission of guilt is punctuated by violent orchestral interjections, then reduced to murmuring tremolos to underpin the chorus's stunned response. The mood is thus prepared for another of Bellini's trademark lyrical pieces ('Qual cor tradisti, qual cor perdesti / quest'ora orrenda ti manifesti ['May this terrible moment now show you / the heart you betrayed and lost'] [26]): again the arpeggios in the upper strings, the sustained violas (later joined by woodwind), the pizzicato bass. And again a vocal melody, led off by Norma, then answered by Pollione, and subsequently decorated by the chorus in parallel thirds, suffused with sighing figures and breathless, sobbing pauses. In spite of its ostensibly sunny major mode, it is made ominous by the repeated 'death figures' in the timpani. After a brief linking passage, the second lyrical number appears ('Deh! non volerli vittime' ['Please don't make them suffer'] [27]), again – almost inevitably – led off by

---

6   Luisa Cambi, *Vincenzo Bellini: Epistolario* (Verona: Mondadori, 1943), p. 297.

Norma, and, of all such numbers in the opera, the most desolate in its minor mode, dragging violin accompaniment figure and solitary horn sonority. However, as the chorus and other characters enter, the music turns to the major and gradually expands into a 'groundswell' figure, still punctuated by agonized, sighing figures from Norma and Pollione, but eventually rising to a compelling ensemble climax, something that, especially when repeated, seems almost like a message of hope. But no such hope is left. To insistent cadential gestures and some last cries from Norma, the Druids cover their priestess with a black veil and the opera comes to a brutal close.

* * *

A Note on the Vocal Roles

Italian opera composers of the *primo ottocento* were unfailingly attentive to the singers who created new roles for them. It was entirely in their best interests to do so. Not only was a well-tailored part likely to make the opera's debut more successful, but there was also the matter of future revivals, which were often driven by singer demand. Bellini was no exception, and in *Norma*, as in all his other operas, he was at pains to craft roles that would flatter the particular singers' strong points and, if possible, minimize their shortcomings. A knowledge of his original singers is, in this sense, a key to understanding the vocal configuration that the opera presents.

The difficulties that could arise if the composer did *not* have sufficient information about a singer's qualities is illustrated by the problems Bellini had with Vincenzo Negrini, his Oroveso. Originally, Bellini had fashioned for Negrini a more substantial role in the drama, in particular with a full-scale aria in Act Two. However, at a late stage it became clear that Negrini was suffering from heart problems and could not be overtaxed. Bellini thus moved some of the role to the opening of the opera (which originally started with a traditional Introduzione featuring the chorus and Pollione's aria), and also making sure that at all moments Oroveso is supported by (in some sections even replaced by) the chorus. In hindsight, one might think it a pity that the opening of Act One was altered in this way, as it serves to lengthen further the drama's already long exposition: but the need to suit the singers was absolute.

A much happier conjunction occurred with Domenico Donzelli, the original Pollione. Bellini's tenor of choice in previous operas had been Giovanni Battista Rubini, a singer with a rather light voice, famed for its extension in the highest register. Donzelli, however, was a very different kind of tenor – a more modern one, with a much reduced range and darker overall quality. In advance of their collaboration on *Norma*, Donzelli wrote Bellini an unusually detailed letter about his capabilities. Although already mentioned in Susan Rutherford's article in this guide, it is worth quoting part of it again here:

> The range, then, of my voice is almost two octaves from low D to high C, singing in chest voice up until G; and it is in this range that I can declaim with equal vigour and sustain the full strength of declamation. From G to high C I can use falsetto, which employed with art and strength can be used as an ornament.[7]

This letter makes us aware that early nineteenth-century voice types often correspond rather badly to our present taxonomies. A range from low C to high G in chest voice sounds to us much more like a baritone tessitura: so Donzelli, particularly with his dark vocal colouring, might today sound to us like a baritone with a falsetto 'extension' into the tenor range – a very strange beast indeed. Needless to say, Bellini followed Donzelli's description to the letter. Witness, for example, the opening of his aria, 'Meco all'altar', which climaxes on high G and then suddenly leaps up to the high C: a perfectly natural leap into falsetto for Donzelli, but a strenuous (or, often, impossible) hurdle for the modern tenor.

We know relatively little about Bellini's relationship with his Adalgisa, who was Giulia Grisi. But it is clear from the part he wrote her, and from the other roles she essayed around this time, that Grisi was a soprano (albeit one with a developed lower range) rather than a mezzo. A few years later, for example, she was the first Elvira in *I puritani*, and frequently sang Norma herself. Time and again in

---

7   Francesco Pastura, *Bellini secondo la storia* (Parma: Guanda, 1959), p. 287.

Norma, Bellini makes this clear: Adalgisa and Norma are required to sing the same lyrical phrases, and – even though Adalgisa typically sings below Norma when they are in rhythmic unison – they are plainly equivalent in range, both having an extension up to high C. There is also the fact that, in dramatic terms, Adalgisa needs to sound *younger* than Norma, something that few mezzos will be able to manage. Quite why, in the later nineteenth and twentieth centuries, it became standard to cast Adalgisa as a mezzo remains something of a mystery. Most mezzos cannot sing the role as Bellini wrote it, and are obliged to alter high notes and even transpose entire numbers. The most likely explanation for the shift to mezzo is that the later nineteenth century saw the emergence of a number of powerful soprano-mezzo couplings (Elisabeth and Eboli in *Don Carlos*; Aida and Amneris in *Aida*; Elsa and Ortrud in *Lohengrin*) into which – despite the music – this pair become absorbed.

About our final singer-role coupling, the legendary Giuditta Pasta as Norma, there has been much writing, some of it of dubious authenticity. Bellini knew Pasta's voice very well as he had already created the role of Amina in *La sonnambula* for her. But it is clear that he also had a close personal relationship with her, and that she was actively involved in the genesis of the opera. In other words, Pasta's personality, musical and otherwise, is painted onto this extraordinary role. The trials and tribulations Bellini had with forging his opera, and in particular the heroine's role, are well documented, perhaps especially in the numerous drafts through which 'Casta Diva' passed, even down to the fact that, at a late stage, it was transposed a whole tone lower, from G major to F major. This was a part that made (and makes) astonishing demands: in the combination of simple, hyperdirect utterance on the one hand and taxing Rossinian coloratura on the other; in its extreme range; and also, perhaps most important, in the extent to which the singer must make some of her greatest effects in simple recitative. Admittedly, Pasta was not without her areas of weakness, perhaps particularly in a certain harshness of tone in the middle register: but even in this respect, Bellini converted a potential weakness into a source of strength, assigning to that register some of the most desolate of his heroine's utterances.

Norma: A Selective Performance History

John Allison

Most performance histories do not set their starting point over a century after its premiere. But when that work is *Norma*, there is a compelling reason for doing so that can be summarized in two words: Maria Callas. Not only was Norma widely acknowledged as Callas's greatest role, it was the great Greek prima donna who single-handedly established new standards by which Bellini's heroine is not only judged but understood; in the words of John Ardoin, 'Callas forced us to demand more from the role'.[1] Callas casts her shadow back right over our perception of the opera's earliest interpreters, and forwards too, since no subsequent singer can have undertaken the part without acknowledging her influence. Many Callas-reared *Norma*-lovers have to some extent remained dissatisfied with every other singer they have subsequently heard in the part, but, equally, without her, *Norma* probably would not have remained the most revered Italian opera of its period.

Introducing the first recording of Bellini's masterpiece he conducted with his wife – Joan Sutherland, the other pre-eminent Norma of the mid-twentieth century – in the title role, Richard Bonynge said: 'The singer who can be a complete Norma probably has never existed – maybe never will exist.'[2] That might be a fair response when confronted with Sutherland even at her

---

1   John Ardoin, *The Callas Legacy: The Complete Guide to Her Recordings on Compact Discs*, 4th ed. (London: Duckworth, 1995), p. 207.

2   Marilyn Horne and Jane Scovell, *The Song Continues* (Fort Worth: Baskerville Publishers, 2004), p. 154.

most stupendous, but there is no reason to suppose that Callas at her peak was less complete than is humanly possible. A multi-faceted part requiring coloratura agility and what would later be described as Wagnerian power, the two bound together with bel canto lyricism, Norma has fair claim to being the hardest role in the mainstream soprano repertory on account of these and of her supreme dramatic demands.

The Gold Standard

Callas sang her first Norma in Florence on 30th November 1948, conducted by Tullio Serafin. It was to be the role of many of her most important debuts, and in May 1950 she took the part with her for her first appearance in Mexico City. She would eventually sing Norma eighteen times at La Scala, the first being on 16th January 1952, the same year as her London debut in the role. Her American debut in Chicago in 1954 would turn out to remain her only per-formance in the city of her most celebrated role, but she was heard more frequently in the part at the Metropolitan Opera, New York, from 1956.

That Covent Garden debut on 8th November 1952 was conducted by Vittorio Gui, and the small part of Clotilde was filled by none other than Joan Sutherland. The recording of this performance is justly celebrated, despite some unevenness in Callas's singing and the fact that Ebe Stignani (the Adalgisa) was winding down her career by this point. Yet still in 1957, Harold Rosenthal was able to write of her once-in-a-generation Norma that he was 'enthralled when she is onstage as with no other artist today... When all is said and done opera is more than singing, it is music drama; and Callas's Norma is a dramatic creation of the highest order... We will tell our children or grandchildren about it.'[3] Many different recordings of Callas singing Norma – two studio versions, the rest captured live – all bear testimony to her questing art.[4] She was a growing artist, and the role grew with her, as documented in Ardoin's *The Callas Legacy*.

---

3   *Opera*, March 1957, p. 190.
4   See Select Discography, p. 167 [Ed.].

As the veteran critic Peter G. Davis has written, 'Callas's Norma really had to be seen as well as heard. The controlled simplicity of her movements seemed an ideal match to her sure musical instincts for moulding Bellini's classically sculptured phrases. Callas often expressed her preference for the bel canto repertory rather than Puccini and his contemporaries, despite the brilliant theatrics of her Tosca. Italian director Sandro Sequi once told Ardoin, "For me she was extremely stylized and classic, yet at the same time human... Verismo made her smaller than she was. Her greater genius was revealed in *Norma*, *Sonnambula*, *Lucia*. This was the classic Callas."' [5]

Norma was also the role Callas performed more than any other – ninety times in eight countries – so Stephen Hastings is right to call it her 'central, career-defining role... it is probably no coincidence that the singer abandoned the operatic stage in 1965, when she realized (after her final performances in Paris) that she could no longer do the role justice'. [6]

It was during the performance of *Norma* on 29th May 1965 at the Paris Opéra that Callas collapsed in a state of exhaustion, having completely changed the operatic world's perception of the part in just over a decade and half. Now, half a century on, Callas's Norma remains the gold standard by which all others are judged, and by which we should perhaps approach even those singers too early to have left recordings.

Pasta, Malibran and Grisi

Norma received its premiere at La Scala, Milan on 26th December 1831, in stage designs by Alessandro Sanquirico and on a triple bill that also included two ballets. The title role was created by Giuditta Pasta, the greatest diva of her day; if some commentators were increasingly to criticize aspects of her vocalism, they never doubted her musicianship or dramatic skills. Bellini thought that she possessed an 'encyclopaedic character' and that he would write

5   Peter G. Davis, 'The Diva Standard. Still', *Opera News*, November 2015, p. 37.
6   Stephen Hastings, 'The Callas Voices', *Opera*, January 2016, p. 36.

a role for her exploiting it. He had already enjoyed the experience of composing the title role *La sonnambula* for her earlier in the same year, and he would soon give her the heroine of *Beatrice di Tenda* too.

Adalgisa was created by Giulia Grisi, the soprano for whom Bellini would also compose Elvira in *I puritani*, and for whom Donizetti would write Norina in *Don Pasquale*. The first Pollione was the tenor Domenico Donzelli, something of a veteran in that he had already created one of the title roles in Rossini's *Torvaldo e Dorliska* in 1815 and sung in one of Beethoven's concerts in Vienna in 1822. Donzelli gave Bellini a detailed account of his voice, with the result that the tessitura is less punishingly high (though high notes are not shirked) than in the roles he composed for his favourite tenor, the elegant Giovanni Battista Rubini, in several other of his operas. The original Oroveso, Vincenzo Negrini, had his limitations (his heart condition prevented Bellini from writing anything too taxing for him), so the part is the least demanding of the four principal roles. *Norma* was performed at La Scala thirty-four times in its first season, and it was given there two hundred and eight times before the end of the nineteenth century.

Before his premature death in 1835, Bellini would hear at least one other great Norma. Maria Malibran stepped into Norma's shoes at La Scala in May 1834, having already assumed the role earlier that year at the San Carlo in Naples, and she went on to sing the part at La Fenice in Venice in early 1835. She was to die in Manchester in 1836, at an even younger age than Bellini, becoming like him the stuff of legend.

Both Malibran and Pasta would probably be described today as mezzo-ish with excellent high notes. The subsequent, twentieth-century custom of assigning Norma to a soprano and Adalgisa to a mezzo is dramatically confusing and has robbed us of Bellini's original conception. Adalgisa ought to be Norma's younger rival, an almost impossible illusion if the singer sounds darker and deeper of timbre, and it is instructive to remember that Giulia Grisi – the first Adalgisa, capable of the coloratura Bellini would write into her part as his Elvira in *I puritani* – was fourteen years younger than Pasta at the time of *Norma*'s premiere. Giulia Grisi would go on (like her sister Giuditta Grisi) to sing both Adalgisa and Norma.

The World Takes to Norma

Less than a month after its La Scala premiere, *Norma* reached the Teatro San Carlo in Naples. At its first performance there, on 20th January 1832, the title role was sung by Giuseppina Ronzi de Begnis, though many of the early San Carlo performances were sung by Malibran, and an early Pollione was Gilbert-Louis Duprez, famous for being the first tenor in an opera performance to sing a high C as a chest note rather than in falsetto (at the Italian premiere of Rossini's *Guglielmo Tell* in 1831). Readers interested in early casting details and dates are referred to the performance data in Herbert Weinstock's study of the composer,[7] but a few highlights are worth mentioning here. Bellini himself supervised the first staging in Bergamo in August 1832, with Pasta, and it was Pasta again who took the title role at the first performance at La Fenice on 26th December 1832, exactly a year after the opera's premiere. Bologna had to wait until 9th November 1833 to see Bellini's no longer quite new hit (*Beatrice di Tenda* had already had its premiere, at La Fenice, in March of that year), when the title role was sung by Giuditta Grisi. Turin and Rome followed in 1834, and *Norma* spread around Italy and indeed the world with the speed one would expect, by the end of the nineteenth century chalking up performances in thirty-five countries and sixteen languages.[8]

The first city abroad to hear *Norma* was Vienna, where it was given (in German) at the Kärntnertortheater on 11th May 1833; two years later, Giuseppina Strepponi, Verdi's future wife, would make her Vienna debut as Adalgisa. But London was not far behind Vienna, and on 20th June 1833 Pasta and Donzelli sang the roles they had originally created at His Majesty's Theatre (the following month

7   Herbert Weinstock, *Vincenzo Bellini: His Life and His Operas* (London: Weidenfeld and Nicolson, 1972), pp. 268–75.

8   Charles Osborne, *The Bel Canto Operas of Rossini, Donizetti and Bellini* (London: Methuen, 1994), p. 338.

they also sang *Norma*, apparently only once, on the Covent Garden stage). Madrid, Berlin and Budapest first heard *Norma* in 1834, and the following year it was the turn of Prague, Lisbon, Barcelona, St Petersburg and Paris (where Giulia Grisi was joined at the Théâtre-Italien by Giovanni Battista Rubini as Pollione and Luigi Lablache as Oroveso).

In 1836, *Norma* spread its wings to the New World, where on 12th February Mexico City became the first venue outside Europe to hear Bellini's masterpiece. It was followed closely by New Orleans (1st April, where the first Norma in the USA was one Signora Pedrotti) and Havana (12th August). *Norma* reached another continent in 1837, being seen in Algiers, the same year that London heard the opera in English for the first time, in a translation by James Robinson Planché, the librettist of Weber's *Oberon*. It continued its progress to Amsterdam and Odessa in 1839, Copenhagen and Moscow in 1840. In 1841 it was heard in Philadelphia and New York, both in an English translation by William Henry Fry, and by the end of that year it had reached Constantinople, apparently becoming the first Italian opera to be heard there. Warsaw staked its claim to the opera in 1843, and South America was soon to follow: Rio de Janeiro (1844), Santiago (1845) and Buenos Aires (1849). Loewenberg's *Annals of Opera* follows the opera's fortunes further, among other places to San Francisco (1851), Sydney (in English, 1852), Cairo (1870) and Cape Town (1875).

Enter Wagner

Richard Wagner, one of Bellini's most ardent admirers, had conducted *Norma* in Magdeburg (where he was music director, and soon to compose *Das Liebesverbot*) as early as 1835, but his performances in Riga (during his next music-directorship) in December 1837 have attracted more attention. The city's German-language newspaper, *Neue Freie Presse*, carried the following notice: 'The undersigned believed that he could not better prove his esteem for the public of this city than by selecting this opera. Among all the operas of Bellini, *Norma* is the one that has the most abundant melodic vein joined to the most profound reality, personal passion. All the adversaries of Italian music render justice to this great score, saying that it speaks to the heart, that this is the opera of genius. And it is for that reason that I invite the public to attend in large numbers. Richard Wagner.'[9] Wagner's minor retouching of Bellini's orchestration (brass parts) in Riga was a small gesture compared to the insertion aria he would compose two years later, early in his Parisian sojourn, in the hope of making an impression there. Written in F major for Oroveso and male chorus, 'Norma il predisse' was declined by the bass Luigi Lablache and published only in 1914.

Prima Donna among Divas

Norma cannot be *Norma* without the soprano at its centre, and any history of performances of Bellini's opera needs to focus on the singers who have excelled in the title role: to a greater or lesser extent, they have all been outstanding singing actresses. Musically and dramatically complex, Bellini's grandiose Druid priestess was summed up by Andrew Porter at the start of his survey of *Norma* in *Opera on Record*: 'Bellini's Norma is one of the most demanding operatic roles ever written. It calls for power, grace in slow cantilena, pure fluent coloratura, stamina, tones both tender and violent, force and intensity of verbal declamation, and a commanding stage presence. Only a soprano who has all these virtues can sustain the role.'[10] Despite these challenges, in the long history of *Norma* – an opera that has never really left the stage, even if its popularity dipped in the early twentieth century – there has been quite a roll-call of singers who have met at least most of its demands.

Pasta, Grisi and Malibran – discussed above – were not the only singers associated with Norma during the opera's earliest years. One of Pasta's students, the English singer Adelaide Kemble, was renowned for her Norma, singing it at La Fenice in 1838 and at Covent Garden (in English) in 1841. In Paris she had become acquainted with

---

9   Quoted in Weinstock, op. cit., p. 524.
10   Andrew Porter, '*Norma*' in Alan Blyth (ed.), *Opera on Record* (London: Hutchinson, 1979), p. 154.

Chopin, and was one of his strongest advocates when he came to London in 1848, where he gave his first public concert at her Eaton Place house; he in turn was delighted to meet Jenny Lind, who the previous year had sung Norma in London (in Italian), a role she had already chosen for her Berlin and Vienna debuts (both in German) and had first sung at the age of twenty-one in Stockholm (in Swedish). Therese Tietjens – born in the year of *Norma*'s premiere – based her career in London and became a leading interpreter of the opera in the 1860s and 1870s; on one occasion, singing it on tour in a cramped Dublin theatre, she rushed to strike the gong to summon the Gauls and missed, hitting instead her Pollione (Antonio Giuglini) on the nose, 'causing instantly a profuse bleeding. The curtain had to be lowered in order that the injured Pollione might recover himself sufficiently to proceed with the act... In spite of the swollen nose, which immediately assumed alarming dimensions, *Norma* was brought to a successful close.'[11]

The earliest recordings of 'Casta Diva' were made around 1900 in Milan, by such singers as Ida Sambo and Romilda Nelli. The first famous soprano to record the aria – though she never sang Norma on stage – was Adelina Patti in 1906; she was aged sixty-three by then and sounds effortful in places. One great artist who recorded the aria (in Berlin in 1908) and who had also been a great exponent of the role on stage was Lilli Lehmann. She had sung the small role of Clotilde in her early Prague seasons forty years earlier and then performed Adalgisa while holding out against all invitations to sing the title role until 1884–85. By that time, Lehmann (whose roles also included Brünnhilde and the Queen of the Night) had mastered Isolde and Leonore, and she said that Norma was 'ten times as exacting as Leonore'.[12] Lehmann also sang the first performance of *Norma* in Metropolitan Opera history in 1890 (in German).

Twentieth-century sopranos of the generation before Callas who excelled as Norma included Ester Mazzoleni and Giannina Arangi-Lombardi. Rosa Ponselle – one of those rare great Normas with

---

11 Luigi Arditi, *My Reminiscences*, ed. Baroness von Zedlitz (London: Skeffington and Son, 1896), pp. 95–6.

12 Quoted by Andrew Porter in *Opera on Record*, op. cit., p. 154.

a truly pure voice – sang the role at the Met in 1927, the first time Bellini's opera had been played there since 1892, and she was to sing it nineteen times in the house. Ponselle also appeared at Covent Garden in 1929 as Norma, the last singer to be heard there in that role until Callas in 1952. At Florence in May 1929, the Norma was Claudia Muzio, partnered by Ebe Stignani's Adalgisa; Stignani also sang alongside Gina Cigna at Bologna in 1935. Cigna, who made the first complete recording of the opera in 1937 (again with Stignani, Vittorio Gui conducting), was also regarded as the 'house Norma' of the Met in the late 1930s, and sang the title role in the San Francisco Opera Company's first staged *Norma* in 1937. The next major Met Norma was Zinka Milanov, star of the house's 1943 revival, still singing it there until the advent of Callas.

Post-Callas, the pre-eminent Norma was of course Joan Sutherland, who is believed to have sung the role more than any other twentieth-century soprano. She made her debut in the part in Vancouver in 1963, and sang it at Covent Garden in 1967 and the Met in 1970 (opposite the Adalgisa of Marilyn Horne – the latter's Met debut, although the two singers were already close collaborators). Sutherland's 1964 recording (under her husband's baton, and also with Horne) was the first on disc to restore 'Casta Diva' to G major from its traditional transposition down to F. Writing of their Covent Garden appearance, Harold Rosenthal said, 'I do not think that Joan Sutherland and Richard Bonynge's gentle, elegiac approach is the correct one. Not only were there long stretches in this performance which were boring... this was the kind of performance which must surely have given the impression to those who did not know the opera that it is not a particularly good piece, and that Bellini was not a dramatic composer.'[13] Nevertheless, Sutherland must be regarded as the pre-eminent Norma of her time, who went on to enjoy huge international success in the role.

Montserrat Caballé deserves credit for finding – albeit it for a brief period only – a kind of Third Way between Callas and Sutherland. The film of her Norma from Orange (1974), with Jon Vickers and Josephine Veasey, has been acknowledged even by the soprano herself

---

13 *Opera*, January 1968, p. 71.

as the greatest single performance of her career. Caballé sang Norma for the first time in Barcelona in 1970 and made her first studio recording of it in 1973. At Covent Garden in 1978, she famously fell out with Grace Bumbry (Adalgisa) over transpositions of the Act Two duet, 'Mira, o Norma'. Andrew Porter picked up the story originally in *The New Yorker*: 'Two prima donnas quarrelled over *Norma*. Montserrat Caballé arrived wanting to sing her big duet with Adalgisa down a tone... Grace Bumbry, the Adalgisa, wanted to sing it in the original keys. A compromise was reached by which Caballé got her way for five of the eight performances and then ceded the title role to Bumbry for the last three. Josephine Veasey stepped in as Adalgisa for the last two performances – while Bumbry prepared for her elevation – and continued in the part, competently but unremarkably, to the end of the run. Bumbry, as Norma, also chose the low keys for the duet – but now, of course, she had the upper line in it.'[14]

Any list of Normas from this period must also include Leyla Gencer, Renata Scotto ('a part that does not seem on reflection to be one she needed to add to her repertory',[15] reported the *New York Times* on an evening that saw her being cat-called by partisans), Cristina Deutekom and Beverley Sills (who first sang the role in Boston in 1971). Rita Hunter, who sang it in San Francisco in 1972, should not be forgotten either, especially as she was one of the sopranos who – in the tradition of Lilli Lehmann and Callas – sang both Brünnhilde and Norma.

Among singers still with us – and in some cases active – mention must be made of the Normas of Rosalind Plowright, Edita Gruberová, Katia Ricciarelli, Gwyneth Jones, Anna Tomowa-Sintow, Nelly Miricioiu, June Anderson, Carol Vaness, Maria Guleghina and Jane Eaglen. The last of these singers, though she enjoyed an all too brief career on stage, recorded Norma under Riccardo Muti shortly after singing the title role at Scottish Opera, from where Hugh Canning was full of admiration: 'The famous sopranos and mezzos I have experienced at Covent Garden – Caballé, Bumbry,

---

14 Reprinted in Andrew Porter, *Music of Three More Seasons, 1977–1980* (New York: Alfred A. Knopf, 1981), p. 219.

15 Donal Henahan, *New York Times*, 23rd September 1981.

Verrett, Margaret Price – had nothing like the equipment at their disposal required by Bellini's taxing vocal line. Eaglen's gleaming timbre may lack Italianate vibrancy and colour – you could say the same of Sutherland – but she has everything else, phenomenal breath control, easy coloratura, thrilling freedom in the upper extension of her soprano, and a new-found darkness in the important lower register.'[16] Remarkably, there is also Mariella Devia, who undertook her first Norma on the day after her sixty-fifth birthday at Bologna's Teatro Comunale in 2013, from where Max Loppert reported: 'The beauty of sound and consummate command of the singing line... were neither luxuriously nor showily displayed; those were never Devia characteristics, and at this point her artistry has become indistinguishable from the unfolding of the music and the drama.'[17]

Her compatriot Cecilia Bartoli surprised many by taking on Norma at Salzburg in 2013, but for the singer herself it was a logical step in her exploration of Malibran territory. She has since recorded it with the Zurich-based period band La Scintilla and appeared in a number of houses in the Moshe Leiser-Patrice Caurier production (see below). For someone who spent the earlier part of her career trying to escape the meaningless and uninformed comparisons that were routinely made between her and Callas, Bartoli gave every impression of marching straight into the tigress's den. But she had made the Druid priestess very much her own, bringing out a gentler side than has often been heard. Never one to understate musically, she has turned her characteristic way of attacking a phrase to dramatic advantage, yet she sings a heavily ornamented 'Casta Diva' (restored to G major, as Sutherland and Bonynge did before) with solemnity and as if in a trance.

But Bartoli's reclamation of the part from the dramatic sopranos who – from the mid-twentieth century at least – have coloured our conception of *Norma* has not discouraged the major sopranos of the current generation, especially Americans, from tackling it. Sondra Radvanovsky tried it out first in smaller Spanish houses before taking it to the Met, San Francisco, Barcelona and

16 *Opera*, June 1993, pp. 732–33.
17 *Opera*, August 2013, p. 1013.

Munich in relatively quick succession. And Angela Meade, hailed as a potential great Norma of the future by the *New York Times* when she sang the role complete for the first time at Caramoor in summer 2010, has now sung it on stage in Washington, New York and Los Angeles.

Seconda Donna or Giovinetta?

Adalgisa, the young novice priestess (a '*giovinetta*', as Norma calls her in their first scene together) who has caught the eye of Pollione, ought dramatically to appear more vulnerable than her rival Norma, and indeed as noted earlier the role was created by Giulia Grisi – a soprano, though one in an era when voice-type distinctions were less rigidly made. But by the end of the nineteenth century the part had become the preserve of mezzos, and in the vast majority of the most important revivals of the twentieth century, Adalgisa was taken by quite heavy voices. Major interpreters of the part have included Ebe Stignani, Bruna Castagna, Giulietta Simionato (who sang opposite Callas in Mexico City in 1950), Fiorenza Cossotto, Fedora Barbieri, Marilyn Horne (whose Adalgisa was closely associated with Sutherland's Norma), Tatyana Troyanos and Agnes Baltsa. Grace Bumbry and Shirley Verrett are two singers (like Grisi and Lehmann) who sang both Norma and Adalgisa in the theatre; much more recently, Carmela Remigio has done the same.

Margherita Rinaldi, who sang Adalgisa to Scotto's first Norma in Florence under Riccardo Muti, was the first important soprano to tackle Adalgisa in modern times. (And mention should be made of Scotto's Decca recording of 'Mira, o Norma' with Mirella Freni as Adalgisa, a wonderful glimpse of a might-have-been pairing.) Muti's recording with Jane Eaglen as Norma was perhaps the first on disc to make the case for a lighter Adalgisa, in this instance Eva Mei, and more lighter-voiced soprano Adalgisas have been heard in recent years, for example Rebeca Olvera in the production with Bartoli (Sumi Jo on the recording).

Pollione and Oroveso

Norma is an opera all about its women, and more than in many operas the men seem to be there as foils. Yet that has hardly stopped many leading tenors and basses from taking the roles of Pollione and Oroveso into their repertories: both on musical grounds, and on account of the starry female company these characters tend to keep, the appeal is obvious. In addition, of all Bellini's tenor roles, Pollione is the one that has held the most appeal for star tenors – the Roman proconsul being a figure who stands his ground and is much less of a 'mummy's boy' than, say, Elvino, the leading tenor in the composer's previous opera, *La sonnambula*. Quite apart from the character himself, that may also reflect the difference between Giovanni Battista Rubini (the composer's favourite tenor) and Domenico Donzelli, who by the time he created Pollione was something of a *tenore di forza*. A century later, by the time *Norma* returned to the regular repertoire in Italy, verismo mannerisms were still very much a part of the tenor arsenal, and although perhaps sopranos and mezzos had already moved on when it came to stylistic consciousness, the new generation of tenors was the last to arrive. Hence the loud lyric (verging on *spinto*) tenors who ruled in Italy at the height of Callas's fame as Norma.

In the previous generation, Francesco Merli had been a leading Pollione of the 1930s, as had Giacomo Lauri-Volpi. Appreciably heavier voices arrived with Mario Del Monaco, Franco Corelli (who puts in a noble showing on the classic 1960 EMI recording alongside Callas and Christa Ludwig) and even Jon Vickers. Carlo Bergonzi sang Pollione at the Met in 1970, and Plácido Domingo succeeded him there (singing his first-ever Pollione) on the opening night of the season in 1981. Of that occasion, Donal Henahan reported in the *New York Times*, 'Mr Domingo made a splendidly heroic figure out of Pollione... His voice was equally heroic, though it was pressed to the limits of its endurance in Pollione's punishing first-act recitative and cavatina.'[18] In more recent years, the demands of the role seem to have been met best by Gregory Kunde, who possesses the

---

18 Donal Henahan, *New York Times*, 23rd September 1981.

flexibility to deliver what might be called heroic bel canto. Reviewing his Pollione at La Fenice, Max Loppert wrote that he executed 'every note *come scritto* with a musicianly fervour and clarity of purpose light years removed from the stock Italian-tenor posturing and puffing familiar in this role'.[19]

If the first Oroveso, Vincenzo Negrini, was not a great success, a more important singer among early exponents of the role was Luigi Lablache (the first Don Pasquale), who, as noted above, sang it even under Wagner in Paris. When it came to portraying the father of Norma and Druid chief – essentially, another operatic cleric – the most celebrated exponents have been the great basses of the mid-twentieth century: Tancredi Pasero (captured in 1937 on the first complete recording), Cesare Siepi, Ezio Pinza, Boris Christoff (who can be heard on the 1953 recording from Trieste, with Callas and Corelli) and Nicola Zaccaria and Nicola Rossi-Lemeni (the Orovesos of the two studio recordings with Callas). More recent and notable Orovesos have included Nicolai Ghiaurov, Ruggero Raimondi, Paul Plishka, Samuel Ramey, Ildar Abdrazakov, Michele Pertusi and Dmitry Belosselskiy.

The Age of the Director

Norma is great music drama – as Wagner recognized when he noted how intimately Bellini's music was connected with the words – especially in its exciting and moving final half-hour. Yet *Norma* has always been seen as a singers' opera, and interventionist stage directors have entered the Bellinian picture relatively recently. The post-Callas productions at Covent Garden (Sutherland-Horne, directed by Sandro Sequi in 1967, and Caballé-Bumbry, directed by Charles Hamilton in 1978) paid little attention to the matters of staging. Even perhaps the first scenically striking *Norma* – La Scala's in December 1972, with Caballé and Cossotto – was not much of a success. Peter Hoffer wrote that, 'Much discussion was provoked by the sets of Mario Ceroli, a well-known sculptor. His abstract set, made entirely of wood, impressive seen on its own... failed

---

19 *Opera*, September 2015, p. 1154

to evoke either the score's mystic spirit, its historical setting or its romantic roots. Overpowering and isolated, it obtruded and got in the way of the music and often of the action.'[20] John Copley's 1987 staging at Covent Garden, musically rewarding thanks not least to John Pritchard in the pit and Margaret Price in the title role, caused Rodney Milnes to remark, 'There was a peculiarly "period" feel to the staging – was this really a *new* production? – as if it were happening some time in the 1950s'.[21]

One of the first instances of *Regietheater* in Bellini appeared in Bonn in 1983. But it marked such a departure that Carl H. Hiller felt it necessary to preface his review as follows: '*Norma* is seldom performed in Germany, and in rare cases when it is, theatres usually choose concert versions. No producer seems to believe that one can convincingly mount it on stage. Not so Jorge Lavelli, who demonstrated... that *Norma* can be a thrilling piece of theatre.' The production, starring Mara Zampieri, updated the plot to more recent times and turned Norma herself into a partisan leader fighting for freedom but in love with the commander of the occupying forces. Hiller concluded that 'Thanks to such new twists this *Norma* became an absorbing drama'.[22]

Two years later, Andrei Serban directed *Norma* at Welsh National Opera in handsome sets by Michael Yeargan that recalled early engravings of Pompeii. The leading ladies were Suzanne Murphy and Kathryn Harries, but Rodney Milnes was impatient with the staging. 'Half-masks were ceaselessly donned and doffed; a stage lift oozing Significance rose and fell; characters entered and exited (usually to other characters' music) before and after their time; there was much eavesdropping; Norma's children were so much in evidence that no one can have been surprised at their existence.'[23] But the detail that stuck in most people's minds was Serban's staging of the opera's proto-*Liebestod*. Hugh Canning later referred back to it, saying, 'In retrospect Andrei Serban's lesbian-feminist immolation with

---

20 *Opera*, March 1973, p. 254.
21 *Opera*, April 1987, p. 452.
22 *Opera*, June 1983, p. 614.
23 *Opera*, May 1985, p. 560.

Norma and Adalgisa mounting the pyre at the end seems somewhat misguided.'[24]

The next major director to tackle *Norma* was Keith Warner, in Bielefeld in 1989, with a production that took the opera into a stark and stylized early twentieth-century world, so in *Regie* terms Ian Judge's conservative staging for Scottish Opera in 1993 (Jane Eaglen and Katherine Ciesinki the leading ladies, John Mauceri the conductor) seemed like a backward step. Hugh Canning was disappointed by the direction but praised the designs by John Gunter and Deirdre Clancy: 'an ingenious set, a half-raked forestage with a track for sliding wall panels which part to reveal a beautiful sacred grove, austere Roman quarters, and Norma's hideaway in the midst of the forest. With Bourbon-restoration interior design features and acres of red velvet this was a truly Romantic vision of this ultra-Romantic opera... I can't recall a more handsome-looking production of *Norma* in this country.'[25]

In a work that still lacks many successful stagings, most directors when confronted with *Norma* have tended to resort to their usual trademarks. Guy Joosten's 2005 Netherlands Opera staging was set 'backstage' in an Italian opera house – and the chorus transformed into a star-struck 'opera public' – a concept rewarded with one of the loudest avalanches of booing ever heard at this address. In Zurich in 2011, Robert Wilson put his one-size-fits-all stamp on Bellini's opera (with Elena Mosuc and Michelle Breedt) yet won the admiration of Horst Koegler: 'It's a prime example of his abstractionist, formal theatre: a succession of scenes in front of a horizon, lit by constantly changing colours illustrating the subtle mood-shifts in Bellini's music,' he wrote. The characters' 'silhouettes made an effect reminiscent of Nijinsky's *L'Après-midi d'un faune*, though without the reference to ancient Greece; they were dressed by Moidele Bickel in imperial robes, like actors in Kabuki theatre... It was not my ultimate *Norma* experience, but it was very different from others that I've encountered over the last

---

24 *Opera*, June 1993, p. 732.

25 *Opera*, June 1993, p. 734.

six decades. I don't remember a single one seducing me as much as this did.'[26]

For the first major British production of *Norma* in almost two decades, Christopher Alden gave Opera North audiences (in a staging subsequently transferred to ENO in 2016) an Industrial Revolution setting, in which the subjugating Roman forces became Victorian industrialists. In the monochrome tones of Charles Edwards's sets and Sue Willmington's costumes, the shrine was a forest shed in which the Druids were first found branding a tree trunk with pagan symbols, and Pollione and Flavio arrived in top hats, Flavio smoking a cigar and practising his golf strokes with a Druid axe. The Dutch soprano Annemarie Kremer had to climb onto that tree trunk to deliver 'Casta Diva', something Callas would never have countenanced, but then the entire cast spent a lot of time groping around on the floor or eavesdropping on the drama – typical of Alden's very physical theatre.

An updating to more recent times looks set – thanks not least to Cecilia Bartoli's involvement, described above – to become one of the most widely seen productions. The *Norma* of her preferred directorial team, Moshe Leise and Patrice Caurier, opened at the Salzburg Whitsun Festival in 2013 and has since been seen at two Salzburg Festivals (2013 and 2015), Zurich and Monte Carlo, with the Edinburgh Festival following in 2016. Continuing a trend for Nazi-era settings, Gaul became occupied Paris, and the Druids La Résistance. Not for the first time, some wondered why underground fighters in the twentieth century would have been in awe of a moon-worshipping priestess, and George Loomis thought that the dispatching of a brutally murdered Flavio to a grave underneath schoolroom floorboards during 'Casta Diva' was 'disturbingly sensationalistic', but added that 'the updating became easy to overlook once... interest shifted to the characters' emotions'.[27]

The most recent production of striking note has been that by the African-American artist Kara Walker, at La Fenice. Max Loppert was disappointed to conclude that her '*Norma* africana', as it was

---

26 *Opera*, June 2011, pp. 699–700.
27 *Opera*, September 2013, p. 1133.

dubbed, did not completely add up, though it was certainly striking. 'Walker's own thoughtful essay in the programme,' he wrote 're-minded us that colonialism – Romans subjugating Gauls – is indeed a major theme in Romani's libretto; and I was certainly prepared to go along with her own stated argument (influenced by Conrad's *Heart of Darkness*) for making the locale African, and more specifically Congolese at the time of Belgian rule... What soon became clear, however, was that under Walker's direction the drama of characters and emotions in conflict proved so tame as to lead one to a single conclusion: her notion of opera staging appeared to devise its insights and ingenuities entirely in terms of visual effect.'[28]

Back to Bellini

Nearly two centuries on, we are only now beginning to get back to a truer understanding of the bel canto world, thanks partly to changes of vocal fashion in singing, but perhaps even more to advances with period instruments. Nothing will ever invalidate the efforts of a conductor such as Tullio Serafin, in charge of both Callas's studio recordings, because for all his cuts and adherence to other hand-me-downs of tradition, he achieved the mixture of grandeur and humanity so central to Bellini's conception. Some of his successors have attempted to correct things – Riccardo Muti for instance, who in rejecting the bad things of tradition has also tended to smother those practices worth saving.

Few great operas have thus been more urgently in need than *Norma* of a period-conscious treatment, and one recording that has answered this call is Bartoli's, which uses the critical edition by Maurizio Biondi and Riccardo Minasi and employs a period-instrument orchestra, Zurich's sprightly La Scintilla. Restoring the composer's dynamic and tempo markings, not to mention adjusting some tonal relationships, this uncut version has rare dramatic thrust, yet the work's inher-ent nobility is never compromised. Under the conductor Giovanni Antonini, things snap and crackle excitingly, but equally he allows Bellini's 'endless' melodies all their wonderful elasticity.

---

28 *Opera*, September 2015, pp. 1153–55.

Something similar has also been achieved by Fabio Biondi and his Europa Galante, as can be heard on the DVD he recorded with June Anderson in Parma in 2001. Encountering the same conductor and ensemble but different singers at Warsaw's Chopin and His Europe festival in 2010, it seemed to me that the score was emerging completely afresh and he had rediscovered a key to the composer: Bellini's Romanticism, nowhere better exemplified than in *Norma*, is after all grounded more than anything in an ecstasy of sound.

Weep, Shudder, Die:
Vincenzo Bellini, *Norma* and Their Admirers

Gary Kahn

There are few opera composers of a level beneath the very first rank who inspire such intense admiration as Vincenzo Bellini; nor are there many operas by such a composer capable of driving opera-lovers to such extreme levels of excitement as *Norma*. Why this should be so is worth exploring. A remark by Bellini himself in 1834, three years after the premiere of *Norma* and one year before his own death at the age of thirty-three, gives some indication of the effect he intended his work to have: 'Through singing, opera must make you weep, shudder, die.'[1]

Many of the admirers of Bellini, and of *Norma* in particular, have been prominent musical figures. Some of their comments are well known, others less so, and an examination of what they have said may help to explain the appeal that Bellini can exert. The fact that among these admirers have been composers as disparate as Wagner, Verdi, Tchaikovsky and Stravinsky says a great deal about the reach and range of Bellini's achievement.

Bellini's *Norma* is regularly cited as representing the peak of the bel canto era and generally regarded as being an extension and refinement of what Rossini and Donizetti had already been writing in that style. What is perhaps not so frequently recognized is Bellini's freedom, especially in *Norma*, from so many of the stock operatic forms and conventions of many other bel canto operas. The opera is not

---

1 Undated letter between May and October 1834 from Bellini to Count Carlo Pepoli, librettist of *I puritani*. See Luisa Cambi (ed.), *Vincenzo Bellini: Epistolario* (Milan: Arnoldo Mondadori, 1943), p. 400.

primarily a vehicle for florid vocal gymnastics, but rather a brilliantly realized and profound music drama in which human expression is paramount. There is a high seriousness within Bellini's operas that is frequently absent from those of many of his contemporaries, and in none perhaps is this more marked than in *Norma*, a work whose combination of nobility and humanity is so profoundly affecting.

A frequently published remark by Bellini which was reported by his lifelong friend Francesco Florimo, describing his close attention to setting texts to music ('to introduce a new genre and a music which should express the text as closely as possible, and provide a unity of its song and drama'[2]), should be regarded with some caution. Florimo embellished (or worse, manufactured) a great deal of their correspondence, but it is clear that Bellini was concerned to combine music and words in an unusually exact manner for the time at which he was writing. He worked slowly and painstakingly with Felice Romani, the foremost librettist of his day, on the texts for all but two of his operas, demanding countless changes from him throughout the compositional process and reworking parts of the text many times. It was a collaboration which Romani himself characterized by saying 'I alone understood his poetic soul, his passionate heart, his wonderful mind',[3] and it was he who described *Norma* as of all their collaborations 'the most beautiful rose in the garland'.[4] Bellini produced relatively few operas in his short life; indeed, Rossini had composed thirty-five and Donizetti thirty-six by the time they reached the age of thirty-three at which Bellini died, having composed ten. Although a much repeated extract from another letter, this time purporting to be from Bellini to Agostino Gallo and explaining his dilatoriness ('I write few operas, not more than one a year, so that I can put into it all I have to give'[5]) is now regarded as spurious, perhaps

2 Francesco Florimo, *Bellini: Memorie e lettere* (Florence: Barbéra, 1882), p. 17.
3 Felice Romani, *Gazzetta Piemontese*, Turin, 1st October 1835.
4 Romani, op. cit., 8th April 1836.
5 Supposedly written about 1829, first published in Florence in 1843 and reprinted many times since, this letter has been exposed as spurious, most thoroughly by Friedrich Lippmann in 'Vincenzo Bellini und die italienische Oper seria seiner Zeit', *Analecta Musicologica* 6 (Cologne, 1969).

a more vivid one in a remark to Florimo ('with my style I vomit blood'[6]) has a directness to it that may recommend its authenticity.

From his first professional opera, *Bianca e Gernando* (later revised as *Bianca e Fernando*), in Naples in 1826 until his final work, *I puritani*, in Paris in 1835, Bellini met with considerable success (only *Zaira* in 1829 and *Beatrice di Tenda* in 1833 were deemed failures). As early as *La straniera* in 1829, he was being hailed in Italy as 'a modern Orpheus', although some commentators, not least those outside Italy, while recognizing his great melodic gifts, were not slow to point to the sparseness of his orchestrations and find fault with these. In fact, it can be argued that it is this very sparseness of orchestration and, to an extent, of harmony as well, which deliberately serves to focus attention on the intricate expression of the solo melodic line so central to Bellini's style. What is of particular interest is that a difference was soon being noted which set Bellini's works apart from those of his contemporaries. His operas were referred to as containing 'declamazione cantata' (sung declamation) or 'canto declamato' (declaimed song). The epithet 'filosofico' (Rossini used it in relation to *I puritani*), implying a degree of high seriousness, was employed in descriptions of them, a recognition that their power lies in being dramatic works for the stage and not just occasions for vocal display by leading singers. It is difficult to conceive of the word being so readily applied to many of the operas written by Rossini or Donizetti at around the same time. And *Norma* was recognized by many from its earliest performances as a supreme example of Bellini's art.

There were of course detractors, and among Bellini's contemporaries were some who dismissed him as a musical lightweight, particularly from the point of view of the more sophisticated ways in which German music had been developing since Beethoven. Robert Schumann wrote of Bellini as 'a butterfly fluttering around the German oak', Heinrich Heine called him 'a sigh in dancing pumps' and Hector Berlioz (who intensely disliked bel canto, describing it as 'a sensual pleasure and nothing more'), perhaps even more unkindly,

---

6   Carmelo Neri: *Vincenzo Bellini Nuovo Epistolario 1819–1835, con documenti inediti* (Catania: Editoriale Agorà, 2005), letter 43, 14th June 1828.

described Bellini as 'a grinning puppet'. Nevertheless, at Bellini's funeral the mourners included Rossini, Ferdinando Paer, Daniel Auber, Fromental Halévy and also the veteran Luigi Cherubini, who threw the first earth into the grave.

The great success Bellini enjoyed led to numerous themes from his operas being adapted for the piano by leading musicians of the time. In 1837, Franz Liszt, Frédéric Chopin, Carl Czerny, Henri Herz, Johan Peter Pixis and Sigismond Thalberg all contributed to *Hexameron*, a set of variations for piano on the march 'Suoni la tromba' from *I puritani*. Sigismond Thalberg wrote a 'Grande fantaisie et variations sur des motifs de l'opéra *Norma*' in 1834, Anton Diabelli three potpourris on airs from *Norma* in 1835 and Liszt his 'Réminiscences de *Norma*' in 1841. And when, in 1877, Lauro Rossi, director of the Collegio di Musica in Naples, sent out invitations to prominent composers to contribute to an album of piano pieces being prepared to commemorate the unveiling of a monument to Bellini in the city in which he had studied, thirty-five composers responded, among them Tchaikovsky, Liszt and Ferdinand Hiller. The resulting *Album per pianoforte alla memoria di Vincenzo Bellini* was published by Ricordi in 1885.

Bellini's early successes had spread rapidly beyond Italy, and in Leipzig in 1834 the twenty-year-old Richard Wagner fell under the spell of the great dramatic soprano Wilhelmine Schröder-Devrient as Romeo in *I Capuleti e i Montecchi*. Bellini's operas made a huge and lasting impression on Wagner, and when the latter took up his first conducting posts in Magdeburg, Königsberg and Riga over the following four years, he chose to conduct performances of *La straniera*, *I Capuleti e i Montecchi*, *I puritani* and *Norma*. The last he especially admired, and it was *Norma* that he chose to conduct at a Riga benefit performance for himself in December 1837 (he conducted eight performances of it that season, as well as ten of *I Capuleti e i Montecchi*; two years later, when in Paris, he also composed an additional bass aria with male chorus for Oroveso). He wrote at the time:

I shall never forget the impression that a Bellini opera only recently made upon me [he was referring to the Leipzig performance of *I Capuleti*], when I was thoroughly satiated with the eternal symbolic tumult of the orchestra and once again encountered the noble simplicity of song.[7]

And of *Norma*, he wrote that it was:

of all Bellini's creations [...] the richest in the profoundly realistic way in which true melody is united with intimate passion.[8]

Wagner went on to express his belief that Germans should not deny themselves the intense pleasure that Bellinian melody provided:

...then we shall learn, particularly in the case of Bellini, that it was pure melody, noble and beautiful song that enchanted us. To cherish this and to believe in it is surely no sin: it is perhaps not even a sin if, before going to sleep, one sends a prayer heavenwards that such melodies and such a way of treating song might for once occur to German composers. Song, song and once again song, ye Germans![9]

It is also not without significance that, for Wagner, Bellini's exceptionally strong interest in the dramatic context of his operas held great appeal. Wagner was later to write scathingly about many aspects of opera that did not conform to his own developing theories of music drama, not least that by Italians, but he never lost his love for Bellini. Even though a well-known reminiscence by the notoriously unreliable Francesco Florimo, who claimed that the elderly Wagner had visited him at the conservatory in Naples in 1880 crying 'Bellini! Bellini!' is unlikely to be true (Wagner scholarship has failed to unearth any reference to the meeting), there are nevertheless more than a dozen references in Cosima Wagner's *Diaries* between 1869 and 1883 in which

---

7 Ernest Newman, *The Life of Richard Wagner 1813–1848* (New York: Alfred A. Knopf, 1937), p. 111.

8 David Kimbell, *Vincenzo Bellini: 'Norma'* (Cambridge: Cambridge University Press, 1998), p. 93.

9 Ibid.

Wagner is recorded as either playing Bellini or speaking admiringly of him. After one evening, on 7th March 1878, Cosima records him playing on his piano at Wahnfried themes from *I Capuleti e i Montecchi*, *La straniera* and *Norma* and saying afterwards:

> I have learned things from them which Brahms & Co. have never learned, and they can be seen in my melodies.[10]

Nor was Wagner alone as a German in his admiration of Bellini. The composer and conductor Ferdinand Hiller, an early associate of Wagner during the latter's time as Kapellmeister in Dresden, stated his feelings for Bellini at considerable length in the late 1870s. He wrote of *Norma* that it is:

> ...suffused by a significant, serious atmosphere. There is scarcely another tragic opera composed by an Italian which is its equal in colouring. Great care was bestowed upon the choral parts as well; many of them have been drawn with penetrating sharpness. [...] The great climax at the end not only has an overwhelming effect, but also has become the prototype, or at least the inspiration, for much that has been created since...[11]

Hiller further pointed out that:

> Bellini had the great good fortune to be able to compose for vocal artists who knew how to heighten the effect of every one of the composer's intentions. In the charming duet in *La sonnambula* (just before the lovers retire ['Son geloso del zeffiro errante']), Grisi and Rubini tossed trills at one another like blossoming roses; their sixths and thirds were sung kisses. No verses by Shakespeare could have been more overwhelming than the well-calculated and well-felt

---

10 *Cosima Wagner's Diaries, Volume Two 1878–1883*, ed. Martin Gregor-Dellin and Dieter Mack, trans. Geoffrey Skelton (London: William Collins & Sons, 1980), p. 35.

11 Herbert Weinstock, *Vincenzo Bellini: His Life and His Operas* (London: Weidenfeld and Nicolson, 1972), p. 412.

solfeggios by Pasta when, as Norma, she began: [final scene of Act One] 'Oh, non tremare, o perfido,' and then flung her scale passage in Pollione's face.[12]

And praise for Bellini was also expressed by other prominent German and Austrian musicians of the time. Johannes Brahms noted with approval a comment by Hermann Levi, the conductor of the first *Parsifal* at Bayreuth, that 'in Bellini's *N[orma]* there are some really quite extraordinary and beautiful things'.[13] Gustav Mahler also confessed that there were some passages of *Norma* that moved him to tears.

Verdi, the great Italian inheritor of and successor to the age of bel canto, expressed familiar reservations about aspects of Bellini's perceived shortcomings with regard to orchestration, but nevertheless greatly admired many of his other qualities. In a letter to Camille Bellaigue in 1898, less than three years before he died, Verdi wrote:

Bellini's harmony and orchestration is poor, it is true [...] but he is rich in feeling, and in a melancholy which is all his own. Even in less known operas, in *Straniera* and *Pirata,* there are long, long melodies such as none before him had written. And what truth and power there is in his declamation – the duet between Pollione and Norma, for instance! What loftiness of idea in the first phrases of the Introduzione, and another, just as sublime, a few bars later, badly orchestrated, but beautiful, heavenly, beyond the reach of any other pen.[14]

Tchaikovsky too, despite sharing the general late-nineteenth-century lack of regard for Bellini's orchestrations, always maintained a great love for the composer. During the 1850s, after his family had moved to St Petersburg and under the influence of the Neapolitan singing teacher Luigi Piccoli, he was carried away by performances of Italian operas, including *Norma* and *La sonnambula*. In 1882, he wrote:

12 Ibid., p. 411.

13 *Brahms: Life and Letters*, selected and annotated by Styra Avins (Oxford: Oxford University Press, 1997), p. 410.

14 Stephen A. Willier, *Vincenzo Bellini: A Research and Information Guide* (New York and London: Routledge, 2nd edition, 2009), p. 31.

I have always felt great sympathy towards Bellini. When I was still a child the emotions which his graceful melodies, always tinged with melancholy, awakened in me were so strong that they made me cry.[15]

And again 1891, in the course of an interview with the *New York Herald* during his visit to America, he said:

Up to this day I hear the melodies of Bellini with tears in my eyes.[16]

In addition, as mentioned above, Tchaikovsky was one of the contributors to the festschrift *Album* that was published in 1885.

By the early twentieth century, however, much of bel canto had become a largely ignored part of the repertory, and *Norma* was performed less and less, especially outside Italy. The dominance of Grand Opera, of Wagner and Verdi and later of Italian verismo had resulted in an absence of performers with the refinement and understanding of the technical requirements of the style. At the Met in New York, for example, there were no performances of *Norma* between those of Lilli Lehmann in 1892 and Rosa Ponselle in 1929, and at Covent Garden none between those of Rosa Ponselle, also in 1929, and Maria Callas in 1952. The demands of the title role itself are ferocious (Lilli Lehmann famously said she found singing all three Brünnhildes easier than one Norma). Nearer to our own time, it was really not until the arrival of Maria Callas that post-war audiences had an opportunity to experience for themselves the true wonder and beauties of Bellini. What Callas brought to Norma, a role she sang on stage no fewer than ninety times, is of course now legendary, and it was doubly fortuitous that her arrival on the operatic scene also coincided with the arrival of the long-playing record. Opera-lovers could now immerse themselves in Bellini at home as well as in the opera house. The superlatives that Callas's performances as Norma evoked show clearly that once a

---

15   Piotr Ilyich Tchaikovsky, letter to Nadezhda von Meck, 7/19 March 1882. See
    Modest Tchaikovsky, *The Life of Piotr Ilyich Tchaikovsky*, Vol. 2 (Moscow:
    Algorithm, 1997), pp. 449–50.

16   *New York Herald*, 27th April 1891.

performer who is equal to the greatness of the role appears, the opera is capable of acquiring untold numbers of new admirers.

There have been others since Callas – notably Joan Sutherland, Montserrat Caballé and most recently Cecilia Bartoli – who have sustained the case for the unique qualities of *Norma*, and we should perhaps be reminded of Ferdinand Hiller's comments on the distinction artists like Pasta and Rubini brought to the work. When Bellini is thus served, *Norma* can take us into the realms of the sublime. Igor Stravinsky said in the second of his 1939–40 Charles Eliot Norton Lectures at Harvard that Bellini 'inherited melody without having even so much as asked for it';[17] in Stravinsky's view he 'was not only far ahead of his own time but so far in advance of our own that it will yet be many years before the music world fully appreciates his genius'.[18] It is to be hoped that we have made significant progress since then. Indeed, the Rossini revival of the last thirty years or so has led to a greater appreciation of the requirements of bel canto and has helped educate performers and audiences alike in the requirements of the genre. A new critical edition published by Ricordi of Bellini's scores is also under way, with the one for *Norma* currently being prepared by Roger Parker.

One of the first important commentators of the twentieth century to proclaim the true greatness of Bellini and of *Norma* was the composer and critic Ildebrando Pizzetti. It was he who wanted to dispel the idea that Bellini's operas were only good in parts and strenuously maintained that no excuses need be made for them. He spoke of the glories of what he called pure song and of how it communicated directly to the human heart. It was Pizzetti who in 1915 wrote of Bellini that 'Here was one who spoke with the voice of God'. This is pitching it pretty high, but it is difficult not to feel sympathy with someone who could also write that 'the man whose eyes do not fill with tears when Norma bids farewell to her children is a mean and paltry wretch'.[19]

---

17   Igor Stravinsky, *Poetics of Music* (Cambridge, Massachusetts and London: Harvard University Press, 16th printing, 2003), p. 40.
18   Stelios Galatopoulos, *Bellini: Life, Times, Music* (London: Sanctuary, 2002), p. 331.
19   Willier, op. cit., p. 115.

Thematic Guide

Themes from the opera have been identified by the numbers in square brackets in the article on the music, pp. 25–41. These numbers are also printed at corresponding points in the libretto, so that the words can be related to the musical themes.

Norma

Tragedia lirica in two acts
by Vincenzo Bellini

Libretto by Felice Romani
after Alexandre Soumet's verse tragedy *Norma*
English translation by Kenneth Chalmers

Norma was first performed at the Teatro alla Scala, Milan, on 26th December 1831. It was first performed in Britain at the King's Theatre, Haymarket, London, on 20th June 1833. The first performance in the United States was at the St Charles Theatre, New Orleans, on 1st April 1836.

THE CHARACTERS

Norma *druidess*	soprano
Pollione *Roman proconsul in Gaul*	tenor
Adalgisa *young priestess at the temple of Irminsul*	soprano*
Oroveso *head of the Druids and Norma's father*	bass
Flavio *friend of Pollione*	tenor
Clotilde *confidante of Norma*	mezzo-soprano
Two children, sons of Norma and Pollione	non-singing roles

Gallic Druids, Bards, Seers, Priestesses, Warriors and Soldiers

The sacred forest and temple of Irminsul in Gaul

* Frequently sung by a mezzo-soprano. For more on this, see Roger Parker's article, pp. 40–41, and John Allison's article, p. 53.

Overture [1, 2]

ATTO PRIMO

Introduzione

*Foresta sacra de' Druidi; in mezzo, la quercia d'Irminsul, al piè della
quale vedesi la pietra druidica che serve d'altare. Colli in distanza sparsi
di selve. È notte; lontani fuochi trapelano dai boschi.*

Scena I

*(Al suono di marcia religiosa difilano le schiere de' Galli, indi la processione
de' Druidi. Per ultimo Oroveso coi maggiori Sacerdoti.)*

OROVESO
>Ite sul colle, o Druidi,   [3]
>ite a spiar ne' cieli
>quando il suo disco argenteo
>la nuova luna sveli;
>ed il primier sorriso
>del virginal suo viso
>tre volte annunzi il mistico
>bronzo sacerdotal.

DRUIDI
>Il sacro vischio a mietere
>Norma verrà?

OROVESO
>   Sì, Norma.

DRUIDI *(con gioia)*
>Verrà, verrà.

Overture [1, 2]

ACT ONE

Introduction

The Druids' holy forest. In the middle is the oak of Irminsul and at the foot of it is the Druids' altar stone. In the distance are wood-covered hills. It is night, and distant fires can be made out in the woods.

Scene 1

(When the sacred march begins, the Gauls' troops file in, followed by the procession of Druids. Last comes Oroveso with the chief priests.)

OROVESO

O Druids, go up onto the hill [3]
and look out into the heavens
for when the silver crescent
of the new moon is revealed;
and let three strokes
of the priests' mystical gong
announce the first smile
from her virginal face.

DRUIDS

Will Norma come
to gather the holy mistletoe?

OROVESO

Yes, Norma will come.

DRUIDS *(joyfully)*
She will come!

(con devota fierezza)

Dell'aura tua profetica,   [4]
terribil Dio, l'informa:
sensi, o Irminsul, le inspira
d'odio ai Romani e d'ira;
sensi che questa infrangano
pace per noi mortal.

OROVESO
Sì: parlerà terribile
da queste querce antiche;
sgombre farà le Gallie
dall'aquile nemiche,
e del suo scudo il suono,
pari al fragor del tuono...

OROVESO, DRUIDI
...nella città dei Cesari
tremendo eccheggerà.

DRUIDI
E del suo scudo il suono, *ecc.*

OROVESO
Pari al fragor del tuono, *ecc.*

(Si allontanano tutti e si perdono nella foresta.)

OROVESO, DRUIDI *(in lontananza)*
Luna, t'affretta a sorgere!
Norma all'altar verrà.
O Luna, t'affretta!

Recitativo e cavatina

Scena II

(Escono da un lato Flavio e Pollione ravvolti nelle loro toghe.)

POLLIONE
Svanir le voci! e dell'orrenda selva
libero è il varco.

(with fervour)

> Fearful god, imbue her
> with your spirit of prophecy.
> O Irminsul, inspire her with feelings
> of anger and hate for the Romans,
> feelings that will shatter this peace
> that is so deadly to us.

[4]

OROVESO
> Yes, he will speak savage words
> from under these ancient oaks,
> he will liberate the Gauls
> from the enemy eagles;
> and the noise of his shield
> will be like thunder...

OROVESO, DRUIDS
> ...fearfully resounding
> in the city of the Caesars.

DRUIDS
> And the noise of his shield, *etc.*

OROVESO
> Like thunder, *etc.*

(They all go off into the forest and disappear from view.)

OROVESO, DRUIDS *(in the distance)*
> O moon, be quick to rise!
> Norma will come to the altar.
> O moon, be quick!

Recitative and Cavatina

Scene 2

(Flavio and Pollione, wrapped in their togas, enter from one side.)

POLLIONE
> The voices have vanished! The way into
> the dreadful wood is clear.

FLAVIO

In quella selva è morte:
Norma tel disse...

POLLIONE

Profferisti un nome
che il cor m'agghiaccia.

FLAVIO

Oh! che di' tu? L'amante!
La madre de' tuoi figli!

POLLIONE

A me non puoi
far tu rampogna, ch'io mertar non senta.
Ma nel mio core è spenta
la prima fiamma, e un dio la spense, un dio
nemico al mio riposo: ai piè mi veggo
l'abisso aperto, e in lui m'avvento io stesso.

FLAVIO

Altra ameresti tu?

POLLIONE

Parla sommesso.
Un'altra, sì: Adalgisa...
Tu la vedrai, fior d'innocenza e riso
di candore e d'amor. Ministra al tempio
di questo dio di sangue, ella v'appare
come raggio di stella in ciel turbato.

FLAVIO

Misero amico! E amato
sei tu del pari?

POLLIONE

Io n'ho fidanza.

FLAVIO

E l'ira
non temi tu di Norma?

FLAVIO

Death waits in that wood,
Norma told you so.

POLLIONE

You have uttered a name
which chills my heart.

FLAVIO

Oh! What do you mean? Your lover!
The mother of your children!

POLLIONE

There is no reproach you can make
which I do not feel I deserve,
but that old passion has died in my heart,
and a god extinguished it, a god
opposed to my peace: I see the abyss open
at my feet and I would throw myself into it.

FLAVIO

Do you love someone else?

POLLIONE

Speak softly.
Yes, there is someone else: Adalgisa.
You will see her, a flower of innocence,
a blossom of sincerity and love. She is a priestess
at the temple of this bloodthirsty god; there she appears
like a shining star in a troubled sky.

FLAVIO

My unhappy friend!
Does she love you in return?

POLLIONE

I'm sure she does.

FLAVIO

But aren't you
afraid of Norma's anger?

POLLIONE

Atroce, orrenda

me la presenta il mio rimorso estremo…
Un sogno…

FLAVIO

Ah! narra.

POLLIONE

In rammentarlo io tremo.

Meco all'altar di Venere   [5]
era Adalgisa in Roma,
cinta di bende candide,
sparsa di fior la chioma;
udia d'Imene i cantici,
vedea fumar gl'incensi,
eran rapiti i sensi
di voluttade e d'amor.

Quando fra noi terribile
viene a locarsi un'ombra:
l'ampio mantel druidico
come un vapor l'ingombra:
cade sull'ara il folgore,
d'un vel si copre il giorno,
muto si spande intorno
un sepolcrale orror.

Più l'adorata vergine
io non mi trovo accanto;
n'odo da lunge un gemito,
misto de' figli al pianto…
ed una voce orribile
echeggia in fondo al tempio:
«Norma così fa scempio
d'amante traditor…»

(Squilla il sacro bronzo. Trombe di dentro.)

POLLIONE

                        In my deep remorse
I imagine it, appalling, terrible.
I dreamed...

FLAVIO

          Tell me.

POLLIONE

                    I tremble when I recall it.
Adalgisa was beside me   [5]
at the altar of Venus in Rome;
she was draped in white veils
with flowers in her hair.
I heard the songs of Hymen,
saw the clouds of incense
and felt enraptured
by pleasure and love.

Then a dreadful shadow
came between us:
a great Druid cloak
covered her like a cloud.
Lightning struck the altar,
the day went dark;
in silence, deathly horror
spread all around.

My beloved virgin
was no longer beside me;
from far away I heard a moan
mixed with the crying of my children,
and a terrible voice
resounded through the temple:
'This is how Norma destroys
her unfaithful lover...'

(The sacred gong sounds. Trumpets are heard in the distance.)

FLAVIO
Odi? I suoi riti a compiere
Norma dal tempio move.

DRUIDI *(di dentro)*
Sorta è la Luna, o druidi;
ite, profani, altrove.

FLAVIO
Vieni.

POLLIONE
Mi lascia.

FLAVIO
Ah, m'ascolta.

POLLIONE
Barbari!

FLAVIO
Fuggiam!

POLLIONE
Io vi preverrò.

FLAVIO
Vieni, fuggiam…
scoprire alcun ti può.

POLLIONE
Traman congiure i barbari,
ma io li preverrò!

FLAVIO
Ah! vieni, fuggiam,
sorprendere alcun ti può.

DRUIDI *(di dentro)*
Ite, profani, altrove.

FLAVIO
Do you hear? Norma is coming
from the temple to carry out the rites.

DRUIDS *(in the distance)*
The moon has risen, Druids;
the uninitiated must leave.

FLAVIO
Come.

POLLIONE
Leave me.

FLAVIO
Listen to me.

POLLIONE
Savages!

FLAVIO
Let's go.

POLLIONE
I'll go first.

FLAVIO
Come, let's go,
someone might see you.

POLLIONE
The savages are conspiring together,
but I shall stop them!

FLAVIO
Come! Let's go,
someone might come upon you.

DRUIDS *(in the distance)*
The uninitiated, go elsewhere.

POLLIONE

Me protegge, me difende   [6]
un poter maggior di loro.
È il pensier di lei che adoro;
è l'amor che m'infiammò.
Di quel dio che a me contende
quella vergine celeste
arderò le rie foreste,
l'empio altare abbatterò.

(Partono rapidamente.)

Coro

Scena III

*(Druidi dal fondo, Sacerdotesse, Guerrieri, Bardi, Eubagi, Sacrificatori,
e in mezzo a tutti Oroveso.)*   [7,8]

DRUIDI, SACERDOTESSE, GUERRIERI, BARDI, EUBAGI, SACRIFICATORI

Norma viene: le cinge la chioma
la verbena ai misteri sacrata;
in sua man come luna falcata
l'aurea falce diffonde splendor.
Ella viene, e la stella di Roma
sbigottita si copre d'un velo;
Irminsul corre i campi del cielo
qual cometa foriera d'orror.

Scena e cavatina

Scena IV

*(Norma in mezzo alle sue ministre. Ha sciolti i capelli, la fronte circondata
di una corona di verbena, ed armata la mano d'una falce d'oro. Si colloca
sulla pietra druidica e volge gli occhi d'intorno come ispirata.)*

NORMA

Sedizïose voci,
voci di guerra àvvi chi alzar si attenta
presso all'ara del dio? V'ha chi presume

POLLIONE
>A power greater than theirs [6]
>protects and defends me;
>it is the thought of the woman I adore,
>it is the love that has inflamed me.
>I shall burn the evil forests
>of that god who is my rival
>for that heavenly maiden,
>and overturn his blasphemous altar.

(They hurry away.)

Chorus

Scene 3

(Enter Druids, Priestesses, Warriors, Bards, Seers and Sacrificers, with Oroveso in the middle.) [7,8]

DRUIDS, PRIESTESSES, WARRIORS, BARDS, SEERS, SACRIFICERS
>Norma is coming: her locks are crowned
>with verbena, sacred to the mysteries;
>like the sickle moon, the golden crescent
>in her hand spreads radiance.
>She is coming, and in terror
>the star of Rome is covered by shadow;
>Irminsul sweeps across the plains of heaven
>like a comet heralding terror.

Scena and Cavatina

Scene 4

(Norma appears surrounded by her attendants. Her hair is loose, her forehead crowned with verbena and in her hand is a golden scythe. She goes to the Druid stone and gazes round as if inspired.)

NORMA
>Do you dare to raise
>voices of rebellion and war
>near the altar of our god? Are there those who presume

dettar responsi alla veggente Norma,
e di Roma affrettar il fato arcano?
Ei non dipende da potere umano.

OROVESO
E fino a quando oppressi
ne vorrai tu? Contaminate assai
non fur le patrie selve e i templi aviti
dall'aquile latine? Omai di Brenno
ozïosa non può starsi la spada.

DRUIDI, GUERRIERI
Si brandisca una volta.

NORMA
                    E infranta cada.
Infranta, sì, se alcun di voi snudarla
anzi tempo pretende. Ancor non sono
della nostra vendetta i dì maturi.
Delle sicambre scuri
sono i pili romani ancor più forti.

OROVESO, DRUIDI, GUERRIERI
E che t'annunzia il dio? Parla: quai sorti?

NORMA
Io ne' volumi arcani
leggo del cielo: in pagine di morte
della superba Roma è scritto il nome...
Ella un giorno morrà; ma non per voi.
Morrà pei vizi suoi;
qual consunta morrà. L'ora aspettate,
l'ora fatal che compia il gran decreto.
Pace v'intìmo... e il sacro vischio io mieto.

(Falcia il vischio: le Sacerdotesse lo raccolgono in canestri di vimini. Norma si avanza e stende le braccia al cielo. La luna splende in tutta la sua luce. Tutti si prostrano.)

to dictate answers to the prophetess Norma,
and to hurry the unknown fate of Rome?
It does not depend on the might of man.

OROVESO
But for how long would you
have us oppressed? Have the woods
of our home and the temples of our ancestors
not been tainted enough by the Roman eagles?
The sword of Brennus cannot remain idle.

DRUIDS, WARRIORS
Let it be raised!

NORMA
                    Ah! it will fall in pieces.
Yes, in pieces, if any of you dares to unsheathe it
before time. The time for our revenge
has not yet arrived.
The Roman spears
are still stronger than the axes of the Sicambri.

OROVESO, DRUIDS, WARRIORS
What has the god revealed to you? Speak, what is to happen?

NORMA
I have read in the secret books
of the heavens: the name of proud Rome
is written on the page of death.
One day she will die, but not through you.
Consumed by her own vices
she will die. Wait for that hour,
the fatal hour when this great decree will be fulfilled.
I counsel peace, and I shall gather the sacred mistletoe.

*(She cuts the mistletoe and the Priestesses collect it in wicker baskets.
Norma walks forward, her arms stretched out to the sky. The moon
shines brightly and everyone kneels.)*

Casta Diva, che inargenti [9]
queste sacre antiche piante,
a noi volgi il bel sembiante
senza nube e senza vel.

OROVESO, DRUIDI, GUERRIERI, SACERDOTESSE
Casta Diva, che inargenti, *ecc.*

NORMA
Tempra, o Diva,
tempra tu de' cori ardenti,
tempra ancor lo zelo audace,
spargi in terra quella pace
che regnar tu fai nel ciel.

OROVESO, DRUIDI, GUERRIERI, SACERDOTESSE
Spargi in terra quella pace
che regnar tu fai nel ciel.

NORMA
Fine al rito; e il sacro bosco
sia disgombro de' profani.
Quando il nume irato e fosco
chiegga il sangue de' Romani,
dal druidico delubro
la mia voce tuonerà.

OROVESO, DRUIDI, GUERRIERI, SACERDOTESSE
Tuoni; e un sol del popol empio
non isfugga al giusto scempio;
e primier da noi percosso
il proconsole cadrà.

NORMA
Sì: cadrà... punirlo io posso...
(Ma... punirlo il cor non sa.)
(Ah! bello a me ritorna [10]
del fido amor primiero;
e contro il mondo intero
difesa a te sarò.

Chaste goddess, as you cast a silver light [9]
on these ancient and sacred trees,
turn your lovely face to us
unclouded and unveiled.

OROVESO, DRUIDS, WARRIORS, PRIESTESSES
Chaste goddess, as you cast a silver light, *etc.*

NORMA
Temper, O goddess,
the bold zeal
of these ardent spirits;
spread upon the earth that peace
which you cause to reign in heaven.

OROVESO, DRUIDS, WARRIORS, PRIESTESSES
Spread upon the earth that peace
which you cause to reign in heaven.

NORMA
Complete the rite, and let the sacred wood
be cleared of all the uninitiated.
When the god, in grim anger,
demands the blood of the Romans
my voice will thunder
from the Druids' temple.

OROVESO, DRUIDS, WARRIORS, PRIESTESSES
Let it thunder, and not one of the wicked nation
will escape the slaughter they deserve.
And the first to fall, struck down by us,
will be the proconsul.

NORMA
He shall fall! I shall punish him...
(But... my heart will not let me.)
(Ah, come back to me, charming, [10]
as in the days of our first, devoted love
and I shall I be your defence
against the whole world.

89

Ah! bello a me ritorna
del raggio tuo sereno;
e vita nel tuo seno,
e patria e cielo avrò.)

OROVESO, DRUIDI, GUERRIERI, SACERDOTESSE
Sei lento, sì, sei lento,
o giorno di vendetta;
ma irato il dio t'affretta
che il Tebro condannò.

NORMA
(Ah! bello a me ritorna, *ecc.*)

OROVESO, DRUIDI, GUERRIERI, SACERDOTESSE
Ma irato il dio t'affretta
che il Tebro condannò.

NORMA
(Ah! riedi ancora
qual eri allora,
quando il cor
ti diedi allora...
ah, riedi a me.)

OROVESO, DRUIDI, GUERRIERI, SACERDOTESSE
O giorno, il dio t'affretta,
che il Tebro condannò.

(Norma parte, e tutti la seguono in ordine.)

Scena e duetto

Scena V

(Entra Adalgisa.)

ADALGISA
Sgombra è la sacra selva;
compiuto il rito... Sospirar non vista
alfin poss'io, qui, dove a me s'offerse
la prima volta quel fatal romano,

Ah, come back to me with
the beauty of your clear gaze;
and on your breast
I shall find life, homeland and heaven.)

OROVESO, DRUIDS, WARRIORS, PRIESTESSES
You are slow to come,
day of vengeance;
but the angry god who has condemned the Tiber
will speed that day.

NORMA
(Ah, come back to me, charming, *etc.*)

OROVESO, DRUIDS, WARRIORS, PRIESTESSES
But the angry god
who has condemned the Tiber will speed that day.

NORMA
(Oh, come back
as you were then,
then, when I gave you
my heart,
oh, come back to me.)

OROVESO, DRUIDS, WARRIORS, PRIESTESSES
The angry god
who has condemned the Tiber will speed that day.

(Norma leaves, and everyone follows her in order.)

Scena and Duet

Scene 5

(Enter Adalgisa.)

ADALGISA
They have left the sacred grove,
the rites are over. At last, unseen,
I can sigh here, where I first
met that fatal Roman,

91

che mi rende rubella al tempio, al dio…
Fosse l'ultima almen! Vano desio!
Irresistibil forza
qui mi trascina… e di quel caro aspetto
il cor si pasce… e di sua cara voce
l'aura che spira mi ripete il suono.

(Corre a prostrarsi sulla pietra d'Irminsul.)

Deh! proteggimi, o Dio: perduta io son,   [11]
gran Dio, abbi pietà,
perduta io son.

Scena VI

(Entrano Flavio e Pollione.)

POLLIONE *(a Flavio)*
Eccola! va', mi lascia,
ragion non odo.

(Flavio parte.)

ADALGISA *(vedendo Pollione, sbigottita)*
                    Oh!… tu qui!

POLLIONE

                              Che veggo!…
Piangevi tu?

ADALGISA
          Pregava. Ah! t'allontana,
pregar mi lascia.

POLLIONE
              Un dio tu preghi atroce,
crudele, avverso al tuo desire e al mio.
O mia diletta! il dio
che invocar devi, è Amor.

ADALGISA *(si allontana da lui)*
                    Amor… deh! taci…
ch'io più non t'oda.

who has made me unfaithful to the temple, to our god...
If that had only been the last time! A vain wish!
An irresistible force
pulls me here and my heart is nourished
by his dear face and the breeze brings back
the sound of his beloved voice.

(She runs to prostrate herself on the stone of Irminsul.)

Oh, protect me, O god,   [11]
I am lost.
Great god, have mercy, I am lost.

Scene 6

(Enter Flavio and Pollione.)

POLLIONE *(to Flavio)*
There she is! Away, leave me:
you cannot persuade me.

(Flavio leaves.)

ADALGISA *(catching sight of Pollione, startled)*
                            Oh! You here!

POLLIONE

                                        What do I see!
Were you crying?

ADALGISA
                        I was praying. Ah, go away,
leave me to pray.

POLLIONE
                        But you pray to a terrible, cruel god,
who is opposed to your wishes and to mine.
O my darling! The god
you must invoke is Love.

ADALGISA *(moving away from him)*
                            Love! Oh, do not say that,
I will not listen to another word.

POLLIONE

E vuoi fuggirmi? e dove
fuggir vuoi tu ch'io non ti segua?

ADALGISA

Al tempio,
ai sacri altari ch'io sposar giurai.

POLLIONE
Gli altari!... e il nostro amor?

ADALGISA

Io l'obbliai.

POLLIONE
Va', crudele; al dio spietato
offri in dono il sangue mio;
tutto, ah! tutto ei sia versato,
ma lasciarti non poss'io:

Sol promessa al dio tu fosti,
ma il tuo core a me si diede.
Ah, non sai quel che mi costi
perch'io mai rinunzi a te.

ADALGISA
Ah! tu pure, ah! tu non sai
quanto costi a me dolente!
All'altare che oltraggiai
lieta andava ed innocente...

Il pensiero al cielo ergea,
e il mio dio vedeva in ciel!
Or per me spergiura e rea
cielo e dio ricopre un vel.

POLLIONE
Ciel più puro e dèi migliori
t'offro in Roma, ov'io mi reco.

ADALGISA (colpita)
Parti forse?

POLLIONE

Do you want to escape from me?
Where could you go that I would not follow?

ADALGISA

To the temple,
to the sacred altars which I have vowed to espouse.

POLLIONE
The altars? And what about our love?

ADALGISA

I have forgotten it.

POLLIONE
Cruel girl, go to your merciless god
and offer the sacrifice of my blood.
Even if it were all shed
I still could not give you up.

You were promised only to your god,
but your heart gave itself to me.
Oh, you do not know what it would cost me
if I ever had to give you up.

ADALGISA
Ah! you too do not know
what sorrow you cost me!
I once went happy and innocent,
to the altar which now I have desecrated.

My thoughts were lifted up to heaven
and in heaven I could see my god!
Now that I have broken my vows and am guilty,
heaven and god are shrouded in a veil.

POLLIONE
I am going to Rome, and there I offer you
a clearer heaven and greater gods.

ADALGISA *(shocked)*
Are you going away, then?

POLLIONE
                    Ai nuovi albori…

ADALGISA
    Parti… ed io?…

POLLIONE
                        Tu vieni meco.
    De' tuoi riti è amor più santo;
    a lui cedi, ah! cedi a me.

ADALGISA *(più commossa)*
    Ah! non dirlo…

POLLIONE
                    Il dirò tanto
    che ascoltato io sia da te.

ADALGISA
    Deh! mi lascia!

POLLIONE
    Ah! deh cedi! Ah, cedi a me!

ADALGISA
    Ah! non posso…
    mi proteggi, o giusto ciel!

POLLIONE
    Abbandonarmi così potresti!
    Adalgisa! Adalgisa!

(con tutta la tenerezza)

    Vieni in Roma, ah! vieni, o cara,   [12]
    dov'è amore, e gioia, e vita:
    inebbriam nostr'alme a gara
    del contento a cui ne invita…

    Voce in cor parlar non senti,
    che promette eterno ben?
    Ah! dà fede a' dolci accenti…
    sposo tuo mi stringi al sen.

POLLIONE

       At daybreak.

ADALGISA
You are going! And what about me?

POLLIONE

          You are coming with me.
Love is more sacred than your vows.
Yield to his voice, oh, yield to me.

ADALGISA *(more touched)*
Oh, do not say that.

POLLIONE

      I shall say it until
you listen to me.

ADALGISA
Please leave me!

POLLIONE
Oh, please surrender to me!

ADALGISA
Oh, I can't…
Protect me, righteous heaven!

POLLIONE
Could you leave me like this?
Adalgisa! Adalgisa!

(with the utmost tenderness)

Come to Rome, oh, come my darling,   [12]
love, happiness and life are there.
Let our hearts be in rapture
with the happiness that calls us.

Can't you hear a voice in your heart
promising eternal joy?
Oh, trust those sweet words
and embrace me as your husband.

ADALGISA
(Ciel! così parlar l'ascolto,
sempre, ovunque, al tempio istesso...
con quegli occhi, con quel volto,
fin sull'ara il veggo impresso...

Ei trionfa del mio pianto,
del mio duol vittoria ottien...
Ciel! mi togli al dolce incanto,
o l'error perdona almen.)

POLLIONE
Adalgisa!

ADALGISA
            Ah, mi risparmi
tua pietà maggior cordoglio.

POLLIONE
Adalgisa! e vuoi lasciarmi?...

ADALGISA
Io... ah!... ah!
Nol poss'io... seguir ti voglio.

POLLIONE
Qui, domani, all'ora istessa,
verrai tu?

ADALGISA
            Ne fo promessa.

POLLIONE
Giura.

ADALGISA
        Giuro.

POLLIONE
            Oh! mio contento!
Ti rammenta...

ADALGISA
(Heavens, I hear him talking like this
always, everywhere, even in the temple.
I see him, with those eyes and that face,
imprinted even on the altar.

He triumphs over my tears
and conquers my grief.
Heaven, save me from this sweet spell
or at least forgive my sin.)

POLLIONE
Adalgisa!

ADALGISA
Please have pity
and spare me further pain.

POLLIONE
Adalgisa! Can you really leave me?

ADALGISA
I... oh!... oh!
Oh, I cannot... I want to go with you.

POLLIONE
Will you come here tomorrow,
at the same time?

ADALGISA
I promise to.

POLLIONE
Swear it.

ADALGISA
I swear it.

POLLIONE
Oh, how happy I am!
You will remember?

ADALGISA
                    Ah! mi rammento...
Al mio dio sarò spergiura,
ma fedele a te sarò.

POLLIONE
L'amor tuo mi rassicura,
e il tuo dio sfidar saprò.

ADALGISA
Sì, fedele a te sarò.

(Partono.)

Scena e terzetto finale

Scena VII

Abitazione di Norma.

Norma, Clotilde e due piccoli fanciulli.

NORMA *(a Clotilde)*
Vanne, e li cela entrambi. Oltre l'usato
io tremo d'abbracciarli...

CLOTILDE
                         E qual ti turba
strano timor che i figli tuoi rigetti?

NORMA
Non so... diversi affetti
strazian quest'alma. Amo in un punto ed odio
i figli miei! Soffro in vederli, e soffro
s'io non li veggo. Non provato mai
sento un diletto ed un dolore insieme
d'esser lor madre.

CLOTILDE
                    E madre sei?

NORMA
                              Nol fossi!

ADALGISA

Oh, I shall remember.
I shall I renounce my god,
but to you I shall I be faithful.

POLLIONE

Your love gives me confidence,
and I shall defy your god.

ADALGISA

Yes, I shall be faithful to you.

(They leave.)

Finale: Scena and Trio

Scene 7

Norma's home.

Norma, Clotilde and her two children.

NORMA *(to Clotilde)*

Go and hide them both. I am more than ever
afraid to embrace them.

CLOTILDE

What strange fear is upsetting you,
to make you reject your children?

NORMA

I don't know... my heart is torn
by conflicting emotions. I love my children but at the same time
I hate them! I suffer to see them, and I suffer
when I do not see them. I feel a joy
never felt before, and sorrow as well,
at being their mother.

CLOTILDE

But you are a mother!

NORMA

If only I weren't!

CLOTILDE
  Qual rio contrasto!

NORMA
                        Immaginar non puossi.
  O mia Clotilde!… richiamato al Tebro
  è Pollïone.

CLOTILDE
                E teco ei parte?

NORMA
                        Ei tace
  il suo pensier. Oh!… s'ei fuggir tentasse…
  e qui lasciarmi?… se obbliar potesse
  questi suoi figli!…

CLOTILDE
                E il credi tu?

NORMA
                        Non l'oso.
  È troppo tormentoso,
  troppo orrendo è un tal dubbio. Alcun s'avanza.
  Va'… li cela.

(Clotilde parte coi fanciulli. Norma li abbraccia.)

Scena VIII

(Entra Adalgisa.)

NORMA
              Adalgisa!

ADALGISA *(da lontano)*
                    (Alma, costanza.)

NORMA
  T'inoltra, o giovinetta,
  t'inoltra. E perché tremi? Udii che grave
  a me segreto palesar tu voglia.

CLOTILDE
  What a terrible conflict!

NORMA
                      You cannot imagine,
  my dear Clotilde. Pollione has been recalled
  to Rome.

CLOTILDE
              But he is taking you with him?

NORMA
                                  He hasn't said
  what he intends. Oh, what if he tried to go
  and leave me here... if he could forget
  his children?

CLOTILDE
              Do you believe he will?

NORMA
                              I don't dare believe it.
  Such apprehensions
  would be too painful, too awful. Someone is coming.
  Go and hide them.

(Clotilde goes off with the children after Norma has embraced them.)

Scene 8

(Enter Adalgisa.)

NORMA
                  Adalgisa!

ADALGISA (while still some distance away)
                          (My heart, be strong.)

NORMA
  Come nearer, my dear.
  Why are you trembling? I heard that you wish
  to reveal some important secret to me.

ADALGISA
È ver... ma, deh! ti spoglia
della celeste austerità che splende
negl'occhi tuoi. Dammi coraggio, ond'io
senza alcun velo ti palesi il core.

(Si prostra.)

NORMA *(la solleva)*
M'abbraccia, e parla. Che t'affligge?

ADALGISA *(dopo un momento di esitazione)*
                              Amore.
Non t'irritar... Lunga stagion pugnai
per soffocarlo... ogni mia forza ei vinse...
ogni rimorso. Ah! tu non sai, pur dianzi
qual giuramento io fea!... fuggir dal tempio...
tradir l'altare a cui son io legata...
abbandonar la patria...

NORMA
                              Ahi! sventurata!
Del tuo primier mattino
già turbato è il sereno?... E come, e quando
nacque tal fiamma in te?

ADALGISA
                              Da un solo sguardo,
da un sol sospiro, nella sacra selva,
a piè dell'ara ov'io pregavo il dio.
Tremai... sul labbro mio
si arrestò la preghiera: e tutta assorta
in quel leggiadro aspetto, un altro cielo
mirar credetti, un altro cielo in lui.

NORMA
(Oh! rimembranza! Io fui   [13]
così rapita al sol mirarlo in volto.)

ADALGISA
Ma... non m'ascolti tu?

ADALGISA
  It's true, but please cast off
  that divine severity
  shining in your eyes. Give me the courage
  to open my heart honestly to you.

(She kneels.)

NORMA *(lifting her up)*
  Embrace me and tell me, what is upsetting you?

ADALGISA *(after a moment's hesitation)*

                                        Love.
  Don't be angry. For a long time I have battled
  to stifle it, but it has conquered all my efforts,
  all my remorse. Oh, you do not know
  what I have sworn just now! To leave the temple,
  to betray the altar to which I am bound,
  leave my homeland...

NORMA
                      Alas, you poor girl!
  Is the peace of your youth
  already disturbed? How and when
  was such passion fired in you?

ADALGISA
                            From one single glance,
  from one single sigh, in the sacred grove,
  before the altar where I was praying to our god.
  I trembled, and the prayer
  died on my lips: I could not tear my eyes
  from that handsome face, and I thought I saw
  another heaven, another heaven in him.

NORMA
  (Oh, memories! I too   [13]
  was entranced like this just by looking at his face.)

ADALGISA
  Aren't you listening to me?

NORMA

Segui, t'ascolto.

ADALGISA

Sola, furtiva, al tempio
io l'aspettai sovente;
ed ogni dì più fervida
crebbe la fiamma ardente.

NORMA

(Io stessa arsi così.)

ADALGISA

Vieni, dicea, concedi
ch'io mi ti prostri ai piedi...

NORMA

(Oh! rimembranza! Io fui così sedotta.)

ADALGISA

...lascia che l'aura spiri
dei dolci tuoi sospiri,
del tuo bel crin le anella,
dammi poter baciar.

NORMA

(Oh! cari accenti!
Così li proferia...
così trovava del mio cor la via.)

ADALGISA

Dolci qual arpa armonica
m'eran le sue parole;
negli occhi suoi sorridere
vedea più bello un sole.

NORMA

(L'incanto suo fu il mio.)

ADALGISA

Io fui perduta, e il sono.

NORMA

                         Go on, I'm listening.

ADALGISA
  Often I would wait for him
  at the temple, alone and in secret;
  and every day my passion
  would grow stronger.

NORMA
  (My passion too burned like this.)

ADALGISA
  Come, he would say,
  let me fall at your feet…

NORMA
  (Memories! This is how I was seduced.)

ADALGISA
  …let me breathe the air
  of your sweet sighs,
  let me kiss
  your lovely curls.

NORMA
                    (Oh those dear words!
  These he spoke to me,
  this is how he found the way to my heart.)

ADALGISA
  To me his words
  were as sweet as the notes of a harp;
  and I could see a lovelier sun
  smiling in his eyes.

NORMA
  (I was charmed in the same way.)

ADALGISA
  1 was lost, and still am.

NORMA

Ah! tergi il pianto.

ADALGISA

D'uopo ho del tuo perdono.

NORMA

Avrò pietade.

ADALGISA

Deh! tu mi reggi e guida…

NORMA

Ah! tergi il pianto.

ADALGISA

…me rassicura o sgrida,
salvami da me stessa,
salvami dal mio cor.

NORMA

Ah! tergi il pianto:
te ancor non lega eterno nodo all'ara.

ADALGISA

Ah! ripeti, o ciel, ripeti
sì lusinghieri accenti.

NORMA

Ah! sì, fa' core, e abbracciami.   [14]
Perdono e ti compiango.
Dai voti tuoi ti libero,
i tuoi legami io frango.
Al caro oggetto unita
vivrai felice ancor.

ADALGISA

Ripeti, o ciel, ripetimi
sì lusinghieri accenti:
per te, per te s'acquetano
i lunghi miei tormenti.

NORMA

Oh, wipe away your tears.

ADALGISA

I need your forgiveness.

NORMA

I shall be merciful.

ADALGISA

Give me your support and guidance.

NORMA

Oh, wipe away your tears.

ADALGISA

Either reassure or rebuke me,
but save me from myself,
save me from my heart.

NORMA

Oh, wipe away your tears:
you are not tied for ever to the altar.

ADALGISA

Ah, say that again, heavens,
say those tempting words again.

NORMA

Ah, yes! Yes, take heart, embrace me.   [14]
I forgive you, and sympathize with you.
I free you from your vows,
I break your bonds.
United with your beloved
once more you will live in happiness.

ADALGISA

Say that again, heavens,
say such tempting words again:
through you my long suffering
is calmed.

Tu rendi a me la vita,
se non è colpa amor.

NORMA
Ma di'... l'amato giovane
quale fra noi si noma?

ADALGISA
Culla non ebbe in Gallia...
Roma gli è patria...

NORMA
                                Roma!
Ed è? prosegui...

Scena IX

(Entra Pollione.)

ADALGISA
                        Il mira.

NORMA
Ei! Pollïon!...

ADALGISA
                    Qual ira!

NORMA
Costui, costui dicesti?...
Ben io compresi?

ADALGISA
                        Ah! sì...

POLLIONE *(inoltrandosi ad Adalgisa)*
Misera te! Che festi?

ADALGISA *(smarrita)*
Io!...

You give life back to me,
if it is not a sin to be in love.

NORMA
Tell me, the young man you love,
which one of us is he?

ADALGISA
He was not born in Gaul;
Rome is his native land…

NORMA
Rome!
Who is he? Continue…

Scene 9

(Enter Pollione.)

ADALGISA
There he is.

NORMA
Him! Pollione!

ADALGISA
How angry you are!

NORMA
Did you say it was him? Him?
Did I understand you?

ADALGISA
Oh, yes…

POLLIONE *(approaching Adalgisa)*
You poor girl! What have you done?

ADALGISA *(confused)*
Me!…

111

NORMA *(a Pollione)*
>   Tremi tu? e per chi?
>   E per chi tu tremi?

(Pollione è confuso, e Norma fremente.)

>   Oh non tremare, o perfido,
>   no, non tremar per lei…
>   Essa non è colpevole,
>   il malfattor tu sei…
>   Trema per te, fellone…
>   pe' figli tuoi… per me.

ADALGISA *(tremante)*
>   Che ascolto!…

(a Norma)

>   Ah! Deh! parla…

(a Pollione)

>   Taci!… t'arretri!… Ohimè!

(Si copre il volto colle mani. Norma l'afferra per un braccio e la costringe a mirar Pollione; egli la segue.)

NORMA
>   Oh! di qual sei tu vittima   [15]
>   crudo e funesto inganno!
>   Pria che costui conoscere
>   t'era il morir men danno.
>   Fonte d'eterne lagrime
>   egli a te pur dischiuse;
>   come il mio cor deluse,
>   l'empio il tuo cor tradì.

POLLIONE
>   Norma! de' tuoi rimproveri
>   segno non farmi adesso.
>   Deh! a questa afflitta vergine
>   sia respirar concesso.

NORMA *(to Pollione)*
> Are you trembling? For whom, then?
> For whom are you trembling?

(Pollione is embarrassed, Norma outraged.)

> O faithless man,
> do not tremble for her.
> She is not guilty,
> you are the wrongdoer;
> tremble for yourself, you traitor,
> and for your children... and for me.

ADALGISA *(in fear)*
> What is she saying?...

(to Norma)

> Oh, please say...

(to Pollione)

> You say nothing! You're retreating! Alas!

(She buries her face in her hands; Norma grabs her by one arm and forces her to look at Pollione.)

NORMA
> Oh, you are the victim   [15]
> of such a bitter, deadly deception!
> It would have been better to die
> than to have known this man.
> He has opened a spring
> of never-ending tears for you;
> just as he deceived my heart
> so this wicked man betrayed yours.

POLLIONE
> Norma, do not make
> your reproaches to me now.
> Please, give this wretched girl
> some respite.

ADALGISA
Oh! qual traspare orribile
dal tuo parlar mistero!
Trema il mio cor di chiedere,
trema d'udire il vero.
Tutta comprendo, o misera,
tutta la mia sventura.

POLLIONE
Copra quest'alma ingenua,
copra nostr'onte un velo.

NORMA
Empio e tant'osi?...

ADALGISA
Essa non ha misura,
s'ei m'ingannò così.

POLLIONE
Giudichi solo il cielo
qual più di noi fallì.

NORMA
Perfido!

POLLIONE *(per allontanarsi)*
Or basti.

NORMA
Fermati.

POLLIONE *(afferra Adalgisa)*
Vieni...

ADALGISA *(dividendosi da lui)*
Mi lascia... scostati!
Sposo sei tu infedele!

POLLIONE
Qual io mi fossi obblio,

(con tutto il fuoco)

ADALGISA
Your mysterious words
reveal such horror!
My heart fears to ask;
it fears to hear the truth.
I understand it all, to my sorrow,
all of my misfortune.

POLLIONE
Let a veil conceal our shame
from that innocent heart.

NORMA
You villain, you dare behave like this!

ADALGISA
There is no end to it
if he has deceived me so.

POLLIONE
Only heaven may judge
which of us has sinned the more.

NORMA
Traitor!

POLLIONE *(about to leave)*
Enough!

NORMA
Stay!

POLLIONE *(clutching Adalgisa)*
Come.

ADALGISA *(evading him)*
Leave me, go away.
You are an unfaithful husband!

POLLIONE
Whatever I once was, I am no longer.

(passionately)

l'amante tuo son io.

ADALGISA
Va', traditor.

POLLIONE
   È mio destino amarti,
destin costei lasciar.

NORMA *(reprimendo il furore)*
Ebben: lo compi… e parti.

(ad Adalgisa)

Seguilo.

ADALGISA *(supplichevole)*
   Ah! no, giammai, pria spirar.

NORMA *(fissando Pollione)*
Vanne, sì: mi lascia, indegno;   [16]
figli obblia, promesse, onore…
Maledetto dal mio sdegno
non godrai d'un empio amore.
Te sull'onde e te sui venti
seguiran mie furie ardenti,
mia vendetta e notte e giorno
ruggirà d'intorno a te.

POLLIONE *(a Norma)*
Fremi pure, e angoscia eterna
pur m'imprechi il tuo furore!
Quest'amor che mi governa
è di te, di me maggiore.

ADALGISA *(supplichevole a Norma)*
Ah! non fia, non fia ch'io costi
al tuo cor sì rio dolore…
Mari e monti sian frapposti
fra me sempre e il traditore.

I am the man who loves you.

ADALGISA
   Go, traitor.

POLLIONE
            It is my fate to love you,
      and my fate to leave her.

NORMA *(choking back her anger)*
      Well then, fulfil it, and go.

(to Adalgisa)

      Go with him.

ADALGISA *(imploring)*
                  No, never. I'd rather die!

NORMA *(looking intently at Pollione)*
      Yes, go; leave me, you despicable man.   [16]
      Forget your children, your promises and your honour.
      Under the curse of my rage
      you shall not enjoy a wicked love.
      My burning rage will pursue you
      over the sea and on the wind.
      Night and day my cry of vengeance
      will roar around you.

POLLIONE *(to Norma)*
      Rage then, and let your anger
      call down eternal torment on me!
      I am ruled by this love
      which is greater than you or me.

ADALGISA *(entreatingly, to Norma)*
      Oh, don't let me be the cause
      of such bitter grief to you;
      let the mountains and seas for ever
      be placed between me and the traitor!

NORMA
Maledetto dal mio sdegno
non godrai d'un empio amore.

ADALGISA
Soffocar saprò i lamenti,
divorare i miei tormenti;

POLLIONE *(a Norma)*
Dio non v'ha che mali inventi
de' miei mali più cocenti...

ADALGISA
Morirò perché ritorno
faccia il crudo ai figli, a te.

POLLIONE
Maledetto io fui quel giorno
che il destin t'offerse a me.
Maledetto io fui per te.

(Squillano i sacri bronzi del tempio. Norma è chiamata ai riti.)

CORO *(di dentro)*
Norma all'ara! in tuon feroce
d'Irminsul tuonò la voce.
Norma, Norma, al sacro altar!

NORMA
Ah! suon di morte!
Va', per te qui pronta ell'è.

ADALGISA
Ah! suon di morte! s'intima a te,
va', per te qui pronta ell'è.

POLLIONE
Ah! qual suon! Sì, la sprezzo,
ma prima mi cadrà il tuo nume al piè.

(Norma respinge d'un braccio Pollione e gli accenna di uscire. Pollione si allontana furente.)

NORMA
Under the curse of my rage,
you shall not enjoy a wicked love.

ADALGISA
I shall stifle my mourning,
swallow my anguish;

POLLIONE *(to Norma)*
No god could think up misfortunes
more painful than mine.

ADALGISA
I shall die to make this cruel man
come back to you and to his children.

POLLIONE
I was cursed that day
when fate brought me you.
I was cursed for your sake.

(The sacred gongs in the temple ring. Norma is called to the rites.)

CHORUS *(off)*
Norma, come to the altar. The voice
of Irminsul has roared.
Norma, Norma, come to the sacred altar!

NORMA
The sound of death.
Go, that is what awaits you.

ADALGISA
The sound of your death is announced.
Go, that is what awaits you.

POLLIONE
Ah! that sound! I do not fear it,
but first I shall destroy your god.

(Norma pushes Pollione away and gestures for him to leave. Pollione storms out.)

ATTO SECONDO

Scena e duetto

Scena I

Interno dell'abitazione di Norma. Da una parte un letto romano coperto di pelle d'orso. I figli di Norma sono addormentati.

(Comparisce Norma con una lampa e un pugnale alla mano. Siede e posa la lampa sopra una tavola. È pallida, contraffatta.)

NORMA *(tutto sottovoce)*
    Dormono entrambi… non vedran la mano   [17]
    che li percuote. Non pentirti, o core;
    viver non ponno. Qui supplizio, e in Roma
    obbrobio avrian, peggior supplizio assai…
    schiavi d'una matrigna. Ah! no: giammai.

(Sorge risoluta.)

    Muoiano, sì. Non posso

(Fa un passo e si ferma.)

    avvicinarmi: un gel mi prende, e in fronte
    mi si solleva il crin… I figli uccido!…
    Teneri figli… in questo sen concetti,   [18]
    da questo sen nutriti… essi pur dianzi
    delizia mia… essi nel cui sorriso
    il perdono del ciel mirar credei.
    Ed io li svenerò!… Di che son rei?

(risoluta)

ACT TWO

Scena and Duet

Scene 1

Inside Norma's home. On one side is a Roman bed covered with bearskins. Norma's children are asleep.

(Norma appears holding a lamp and a knife. She sits down and places the lamp on a table. She is pale and distraught.)

NORMA *(very quietly)*
    They are both asleep. They shall not see the hand   [17]
    which strikes them. O my heart, feel no remorse;
    they cannot live. Here they would suffer torture and in Rome
    disgrace, a much worse torture:
    the slaves of a stepmother. Oh, no, never.

(She gets up, resolute.)

    Yes, they shall die.

(She moves forward and then stops.)

    I cannot go near them;
    I feel chilled and my hair
    stands on end. Kill my children!   [18]
    My dear, dear children; a moment ago
    they were my delight, in their smiles
    I thought I saw the forgiveness of heaven...
    How can I kill them? What have they done wrong?

(determined)

Di Pollïon son figli:
ecco il delitto. Essi per me son morti;
muoian per lui: n'abbia rimorso il crudo,
n'abbia rimorso, anche all'amante in braccio,
e non sia pena che la sua somigli.
Feriam...

(S'incammina verso il letto; alza il pugnale; dà un grido inorridita.)

      Ah no!...

(Al grido i fanciulli si svegliano.)

             Son figli miei!... Miei figli!

(Norma li abbraccia piangendo amaramente.)

    Olà!... Clotilde!

Scena II

(Sorte Clotilde.)

NORMA
          Vola...
Adalgisa a me guida.

CLOTILDE
           Ella qui presso
solitaria s'aggira, e prega, e plora.

NORMA
Va'.

(Clotilde parte.)

    Si emendi il mio fallo... e poi... si mora.

Scena III

ADALGISA *(sortendo, con timore)*
Me chiami, o Norma!...

(sbigottita)

They are Pollione's children:
that is their crime. Through me they shall die;
let them die for him – let that cruel man feel remorse,
let him feel remorse, even as he embraces his lover –
and there will be no grief like his.
Strike!

(She goes towards the bed, raises the knife, then lets out a cry of horror.)

Oh no!

(At this cry the children wake up.)

They are my children! My children!

(Norma embraces them as she weeps bitterly.)

Clotilde!

Scene 2

(Enter Clotilde.)

NORMA

Go quickly
and bring Adalgisa to me.

CLOTILDE

She is here, close by,
wandering alone, praying and weeping.

NORMA

Go.

(Clotilde leaves.)

Let me atone for my sin, and then die.

Scene 3

ADALGISA *(entering, timidly)*
You called me, Norma?

(in dismay)

Qual ti copre il volto

tristo pallor?

NORMA

Pallor di morte. Io tutta
l'onta mia ti rivelo. A me prostrata
eri tu dianzi... a te mi prostro adesso,
e questi figli... e sai di chi son figli...
nelle tue braccia io pongo.

ADALGISA

O sventurati,

o innocenti fanciulli!

NORMA

Ah! sì... li piangi...
Se tu sapessi!... ma infernal segreto
ti si nasconda. Una preghiera sola
odi, e l'adempi, se pietà pur merta
il presente mio duol... e il duol futuro.

ADALGISA

Tutto, tutto io prometto.

NORMA

Il giura.

ADALGISA

Il giuro.

NORMA

Odi. Purgar quest'aura
contaminata dalla mia presenza
ho risoluto; né trar meco io posso
quest'infelici: a te li affido...

ADALGISA

Oh ciel!

A me li affidi?

Why is your face
so pale and sad?

NORMA

It is the pallor of death. I shall reveal to you
all my shame. You were kneeling in front of me
before... now I am kneeling in front of you,
and these children... and you know whose children they are...
I entrust into your arms.

ADALGISA

Oh, poor things,
innocent children!

NORMA

Yes, you pity them...
If only you knew!... but a horrible secret
must be kept from you. Listen to one single request,
and carry it out, if my present grief
and my grief to come are worthy of pity.

ADALGISA

I promise to do everything.

NORMA

Swear it.

ADALGISA

I swear it.

NORMA

Listen, I have decided
to cleanse this air tainted by my presence.
I cannot take these poor souls
with me: I entrust them to you.

ADALGISA

Heavens!
You entrust them to me?

NORMA
>   Nel romano campo
> guidali a lui, che nominar non oso.

ADALGISA
> Oh! che mai chiedi?

NORMA
>   Sposo
> ti sia men crudo... Io gli perdono, e moro.

ADALGISA
> Sposo!... Ah! mai...

NORMA
>   Pei figli suoi t'imploro.
> Deh! con te, con te li prendi...   [19]
> li sostieni, li difendi...
> non ti chiedo onori e fasci;
> a' tuoi figli ei fian serbati:
> prego sol che i miei non lasci
> schiavi, abbietti, abbandonati...
> Basti a te che disprezzata,
> che tradita io fui per te.
> Adalgisa, deh! ti mova
> tanto strazio del mio cor.

ADALGISA
> Norma! ah! Norma! Ancora amata,
> madre ancor sarai per me.
> Tienti i figli. Ah! non fia mai
> ch'io mi tolga a queste arene.

NORMA
> Tu giurasti...

ADALGISA
>   Sì, giurai...
> ma il tuo bene, il sol tuo bene.
> Vado al campo, ed all'ingrato
> tutti io reco i tuoi lamenti.

NORMA
Take them to the Roman camp,
to the man whose name I cannot mention.

ADALGISA
Oh, what are you asking?

NORMA
I hope he will be
less cruel a husband to you; I forgive him, and shall die.

ADALGISA
Husband! No, never!

NORMA
I beg you, for his children's sake.
Please, take them with you,   [19]
support them and protect them;
I am not asking you for honour and power,
let that be for your own children.
I ask only that you do not abandon mine
to slavery, degradation and neglect.
It is enough that I was scorned
and betrayed for you.
Adalgisa, please be moved
by the suffering in my heart.

ADALGISA
Oh, Norma, through me
you will again be a beloved mother.
Keep your children. I shall never
leave this land.

NORMA
You swore…

ADALGISA
Yes, I swore,
but only to do what was good for you.
I shall go to the camp and tell
the ungrateful man of all your grief.

La pietà che m'hai destato
parlerà sublimi accenti...
Spera, ah ! spera, amor, natura
ridestarsi in lui vedrai...
Del suo cor son io secura...
Norma ancor vi regnerà, *ecc.*

NORMA

Ch'io lo preghi? Ah! no: giammai.

ADALGISA

Norma, ti piega.

NORMA

No, più non t'odo. Parti... va'...

ADALGISA

Ah! no: giammai! Ah! no.
Mira, o Norma, a' tuoi ginocchi   [20]
questi cari pargoletti.
Ah! pietà di lor ti tocchi,
se non hai di te pietà.

NORMA

Ah! perché la mia costanza
vuoi scemar con molli affetti?
Più lusinghe, ah! più speranza,
presso a morte un cor non ha.

ADALGISA

Mira questi cari pargoletti,
questi cari, ah! li vedi, ah!

NORMA

Ah! perché la vuoi scemar, ah!
Ah! perché la mia costanza, *ecc.*

ADALGISA

Mira, o Norma, a' tuoi ginocchi, *ecc.*
Cedi... deh! cedi!

The pity you have roused in me
will speak with sublime words.
Oh, keep the hope that you will see
love and nature born again in him.
I am certain of his feelings,
Norma will reign once more in his heart, *etc.*

NORMA
Shall I beg him? Oh, no, never!

ADALGISA
Norma, do as I ask.

NORMA
No, I shall not listen any more to you. Leave me, go.

ADALGISA
Oh, no, never. Oh, no.
Norma, look at these dear children   [20]
of yours at your knees.
Be moved by pity for them,
even if you have no pity for yourself.

NORMA
Oh, why do you want to undermine
my resolve with soft sentiment?
When a heart is close to death
it has no more illusions, no more hope.

ADALGISA
Look at these dear children,
see these dear ones!

NORMA
Oh, why do you want to undermine it?
Oh, why do you want to undermine my resolve, *etc.*

ADALGISA
Norma, look at these dear children, *etc.*
Please give way!

NORMA

               Ah! lasciami…
Ei t'ama.

ADALGISA

      E già sen pente.

NORMA

E tu?…

ADALGISA

      L'amai… quest'anima
sol l'amistade or sente.

NORMA

O giovinetta!… E vuoi…

ADALGISA

Renderti i dritti tuoi,
o teco al cielo e agli uomini
giuro celarmi ognor.

NORMA

Hai vinto… hai vinto… Abbracciami.
Trovo un'amica ancor.

NORMA, ADALGISA

Sì, fino all'ore estreme   [21]
compagna tua m'avrai;
per ricovrarci insieme
ampia è la terra assai.
Teco del fato all'onte
ferma opporrò la fronte,
finché il tuo core a battere
io senta sul mio cor.

(Partono.)

Coro e scena

Scena IV

*Luogo solitario presso il bosco dei Druidi, cinto da burroni e da caverne.
In fondo un lago attraversato da un ponte di pietra.*

NORMA
Oh, leave me.
He loves you.

ADALGISA
He has already changed his mind.

NORMA
And you?

ADALGISA
I used to love him. Now my heart
feels only friendship for him.

NORMA
Oh, my dear girl! What is it you want?

ADALGISA
To restore what is rightly yours
or else I swear by heaven and men
to stay concealed with you for ever.

NORMA
Yes, you have won. Embrace me.
I find in you again a friend.

NORMA, ADALGISA
Yes, you will have me as your friend   [21]
until your last hour;
the world is large enough
to be a shelter to both of us together.
With you I shall set my face firmly
against the shame which fate may bring,
as long as I feel your heart
beating on mine.

(They leave.)

Chorus and Scena

Scene 4

*A deserted place near the Druids' wood, ringed by ravines and caves.
At the back is a lake, which is crossed by a stone bridge.*

GUERRIERI GALLI *(con mistero)*

Non partì?...   [22]

                    Finora è al campo.
Tutto il dice: i feri carmi,
il fragor, il suon dell'armi,
dell'insegne il ventilar.
Attendiam: un breve inciampo
non ci turbi, non ci arresti;
e in silenzio il cor s'appresti
la grand'opra a consumar.

Scena V

OROVESO *(entrando)*

Guerrieri! a voi venirne
credea foriero d'avvenir migliore.
Il generoso ardore,
l'ira che in sen vi bolle
io credea secondar; ma il dio non volle.

GUERRIERI

Come? Le nostre selve
l'abborrito proconsole non lascia?
Non riede al Tebro?

OROVESO

                          Un più temuto e fiero
latino condottiero
a Pollïon succede, e di novelle
possenti legïoni
afforza il campo che ne tien prigioni.

GUERRIERI

E Norma il sa? Di pace
è consigliera ancor?

OROVESO

                    Invan di Norma
la mente investigai: sembra che il nume
più non favelli a lei, che oblio la prenda
dell'universo.

GALLIC WARRIORS *(mysteriously)*
  Has he not left?
  [22]
              He is still in the camp.
  Everything indicates it: the bold singing,
  the noise, the sound of arms,
  the waving of flags.
  Let us wait: a short delay
  will not put us off or halt us.
  And in silence let our hearts prepare
  to carry out this great task.

Scene 5

OROVESO *(entering)*
  Soldiers! I thought I would
  be coming to you with news of a better future.
  I hoped to encourage your passions,
  the anger burning in your breasts.
  But our god did not want it so.

WARRIORS
  What? Is the loathed proconsul
  not leaving our forests?
  Is he not going back to the Tiber?

OROVESO
                    A more fearsome and proud
  Roman commander
  is to succeed Pollione, and he is reinforcing
  the camp in which we are imprisoned
  with powerful legions.

WARRIORS
  Does Norma know this? Does she
  still advise peace?

OROVESO
              I questioned Norma
  to no avail: it is as if the god
  no longer speaks to her, and she is forgetful
  of the whole world.

GUERRIERI

      E che far pensi?

OROVESO

                Al fato

piegar la fronte, separarci, e nullo
lasciar sospetto del fallito intento.

GUERRIERI

E finger sempre?

OROVESO

         Cruda legge! il sento.

(con ferocia)

Ah! del Tebro al giogo indegno   [23]
fremo io pure, all'armi anelo;
ma nemico è sempre il cielo,
ma consiglio è simular.

GUERRIERI

Sì, fingiam, se il finger giovi;
ma il furor in sen si covi.

OROVESO

Divoriam in cor lo sdegno,
tal che Roma estinto il creda.
Dì verrà, che desto ei rieda
più tremendo a divampar.

GUERRIERI

Guai per Roma allor che il segno
dia dell'armi il sacro altar!
Sì, fingiam, se il finger giovi,
ma il furore in sen si covi.

(Partono.)

Finale dell'Atto II

Scena VI

Tempio d'Irminsul. Ara da un lato.

134

WARRIORS

What do you think we should do?

OROVESO

Bow

to fate, separate, and arouse
no suspicion of our failed intention.

WARRIORS
Must we always pretend?

OROVESO

It is a cruel command, I know.

(fiercely)

I too rage at being   [23]
under the Roman yoke, and long for battle.
But heaven is always against us
and pretence is advised.

WARRIORS
Yes, let us pretend if we must;
but let fury smoulder in our breasts.

OROVESO
Let us swallow the anger in our hearts
so that Rome thinks it has died.
But the day will come when it will waken
and return blazing more fiercely.

WARRIORS
Woe betide Rome when the altar
gives the signal for battle!
Yes, let us pretend if we must,
but let fury smoulder in our breasts.

(They leave.)

Act Two Finale

Scene 6

The temple of Irminsul. The altar is to one side.

NORMA
Ei tornerà. Sì, mia fidanza è posta
in Adalgisa: ei tornerà pentito,
supplichevole, amante. Oh! a tal pensiero
sparisce il nuvol nero
che mi premea la fronte, e il sol m'arride,
come del primo amore ai dì felici.

(Esce Clotilde.)

Clotilde!

CLOTILDE
        O Norma!... Uopo è d'ardir.

NORMA
                          Che dici?

CLOTILDE
Lassa!

NORMA
    Favella.

CLOTILDE
         Indarno
parlò Adalgisa, e pianse.

NORMA
                  Ed io fidarmi
di lei dovea? Di mano uscirmi, e bella
del suo dolore, presentarsi all'empio
ella tramava.

CLOTILDE
           Ella ritorna al tempio.
Trista, dolente, implora
di profferir suoi voti.

NORMA
          Ed egli?

CLOTILDE
                 Ed egli
rapirla giura anco all'altar del nume.

NORMA
    He will come back. Yes, I place my trust
    in Adalgisa: he will come back repentant,
    imploring, full of love. That thought
    sweeps away the black cloud
    hanging over my head, and the sun smiles on me
    as on those happy days when we were first in love.

(Enter Clotilde.)

    Clotilde!

CLOTILDE
            Norma! You must have courage!

NORMA
                                What are you saying?

CLOTILDE
    Alas!

NORMA
        Speak.

CLOTILDE
            Adalgisa spoke
    and wept in vain.

NORMA
                Should I have
    trusted her? She was planning to escape me
    and go to the villain,
    lovely in her distress.

CLOTILDE
                    She is going back to the temple.
    Sad and mournful, she is begging
    to take her vows.

NORMA
                And he?

CLOTILDE
                    He has sworn
    to abduct her even from the altar of our god.

NORMA
> Troppo il fellon presume.
> Lo previen mia vendetta, e qui di sangue...
> sangue romano... scorreran torrenti.

(Norma corre all'ara e batte tre volte lo scudo d'Irminsul. Trombe di dentro.)

OROVESO, SACERDOTESSE, DRUIDI *(di dentro)*
> Squilla il bronzo del dio!

Scena VII

(Accorrono da varie parti Oroveso, i Druidi, i Bardi e le Ministre. Norma si colloca sull'altare.)

OROVESO, DRUIDI, SACERDOTESSE
> Norma! che fu? Percosso
> lo scudo d'Irminsul, quali alla terra
> decreti intìma?

NORMA
>   Guerra,
> strage, sterminio.

OROVESO, DRUIDI, SACERDOTESSE
>   A noi pur dianzi pace
> s'imponea pel tuo labbro!

NORMA
>   Ed ira adesso,
> stragi, furore e morti.
> Il cantico di guerra alzate, o forti.

OROVESO, DRUIDI, SACERDOTESSE
> Guerra, guerra! Le galliche selve   [24]
> quante han querce producon guerrier.
> Qual sui greggi fameliche belve,
> sui Romani van essi a cader.
> Sangue, sangue! Le galliche scuri
> fino al tronco bagnate ne son.

NORMA
The villain is too bold.
My vengeance will forestall him, and torrents
of Roman blood will be shed here.

*(Norma runs to the altar and strikes the shield of Irminsul three times.
Trumpets sound in the distance.)*

OROVESO, DRUIDS, PRIESTESSES *(in the distance)*
The gong of our god is sounding!

Scene 7

*(Oroveso, the Druids, Bards and Priestesses run in from all directions.
Norma takes up her place at the altar.)*

OROVESO, DRUIDS, PRIESTESSES
Norma! What has happened?
What news does the striking of Irminsul's shield
bring to this land?

NORMA
                    War,
slaughter, annihilation.

OROVESO, DRUIDS, PRIESTESSES
                    But it is no time since you yourself
bade us keep peace!

NORMA
                    And now I speak of anger,
slaughter, fury and corpses.
Men, raise the hymn of war.

OROVESO, DRUIDS, PRIESTESSES
War, war! The forests of Gaul   [24]
bring forth as many soldiers as there are trees.
As ravenous beasts fall upon the flocks
so may the soldiers fall on the Romans.
Blood, blood! Let the Gauls' axes
be soaked to the hilt in Roman blood.

Sovra i flutti del Ligeri impuri
ei gorgoglia con funebre suon.
Strage, strage, sterminio, vendetta!
già comincia, si compie, s'affretta.
Come biade da falci mietute
son di Roma le schiere cadute.
Tronchi i vanni, recisi gli artigli,
abbattuta ecco l'aquila al suol.

(con Norma)

A mirare il trionfo de' figli
ecco il dio sovra un raggio di sol.

OROVESO
Né compi il rito, o Norma?
né la vittima accenni?

NORMA
           Ella fia pronta.
Non mai l'altar tremendo
di vittime mancò... Ma qual tumulto?

Scena VIII

CLOTILDE *(entrando, frettolosa)*
Al nostro tempio insulto
fece un Romano: nella sacra chiostra
delle vergini alunne egli fu colto.

OROVESO, DRUIDI, SACERDOTESSE
Un Romano?

NORMA
         (Che ascolto?
Se mai foss'egli?)

OROVESO, DRUIDI, SACERDOTESSE
          A noi vien tratto.

NORMA
              (È desso!)

It will bubble grimly
on the polluted waves of the Loire
Slaughter, extermination, revenge
has begun and will quickly be accomplished.
The Roman troops will fall
like corn mown down by scythes.
With its wings broken and its claws clipped,
see the eagle cast to the ground.

(with Norma)

Behold our god, watching
his sons' victory, on a ray of sunshine.

OROVESO
Will you not perform the rites, Norma?
Will you not indicate the victim?

NORMA

The victim is at hand.
Our great altar has never lacked
for victims… What is this noise?

Scene 8

CLOTILDE *(hurrying in)*
A Roman has desecrated our temple.
He was caught in the sacred cloister
of the virgin novices.

OROVESO, DRUIDS, PRIESTESSES
A Roman?

NORMA
(What am I hearing?
What if it is him?)

OROVESO, DRUIDS, PRIESTESSES
Bring him to us.

NORMA

(It is him!)

Scena IX

(Entra Pollione, condotto da due guerrieri.)

OROVESO, DRUIDI, SACERDOTESSE
È Pollïon!

NORMA
      (Son vendicata adesso!)

OROVESO *(a Pollione)*
Sacrilego nemico, e che ti spinse
a vïolar queste temute soglie,
a sfidar l'ira d'Irminsul?

POLLIONE *(con fierezza)*
             Ferisci!
Ma non interrogarmi.

NORMA *(svelandosi)*
           Io ferir deggio.
Scostatevi.

POLLIONE
      Chi veggio?
Norma!

NORMA
      Sì, Norma.

OROVESO, DRUIDI, SACERDOTESSE
          Il sacro ferro impugna,
vendica il tempio e il dio.

NORMA *(prende il pugnale dalle mani di Oroveso)*
Sì, feriamo…

(Si arresta.)

OROVESO, DRUIDI, SACERDOTESSE
      Ah, tu tremi?

Scene 9

(Two soldiers escort Pollione in.)

OROVESO, DRUIDS, PRIESTESSES
It's Pollione!

NORMA
(Now I have my revenge.)

OROVESO *(to Pollione)*
Blasphemer and enemy, what made you
violate this fearful threshold
and defy the anger of Irminsul?

POLLIONE *(proudly)*
Kill me,
but do not question me.

NORMA *(revealing herself)*
I shall strike him.
Stand aside.

POLLIONE
Whom do I see?
Norma!

NORMA
Yes, Norma.

OROVESO, DRUIDS, PRIESTESSES
Take the sacred knife
and avenge our god.

NORMA *(taking the knife from Oroveso's hands)*
Yes, let me strike…

(She stops.)

OROVESO, DRUIDS, PRIESTESSES
Are you trembling?

NORMA

(Ah! non poss'io.)

OROVESO, DRUIDI, SACERDOTESSE
Che fia? Perché t'arresti?

NORMA
(Poss'io sentir pietà?)

OROVESO, DRUIDI, SACERDOTESSE
Ferisci.

NORMA

Io deggio
interrogarlo... investigar qual sia
l'insidïata e complice ministra
che il profan persuase a fallo estremo.
Ite per poco.

OROVESO, DRUIDI, SACERDOTESSE *(allontanandosi)*
(Che far pensa?)

POLLIONE

(Io fremo.)

(Oroveso e il Coro si ritirano. Il tempio rimane sgombro.)

Scena X

NORMA
In mia man alfin tu sei;   [25]
niun potria spezzar tuoi nodi.
Io lo posso.

POLLIONE
Tu nol déi.

NORMA
Io lo voglio.

POLLIONE
Come?

NORMA

(Oh, I cannot do it.)

OROVESO, DRUIDS, PRIESTESSES
What is this? Why did you stop?

NORMA
(Can I really feel mercy?)

OROVESO, DRUIDS, PRIESTESSES
Strike.

NORMA

I have to
question him, and discover which priestess
was enticed into being his accomplice
and led this profaner to commit this worst of crimes.
Leave us for a while.

OROVESO, DRUIDS, PRIESTESSES *(as they go)*
(What does she intend to do?)

POLLIONE

(I am afraid.)

(Oroveso and the Chorus withdraw, leaving the temple deserted.)

Scene 10

NORMA
At last you are in my hands,   [25]
no one can cut your bonds.
I can.

POLLIONE
You must not.

NORMA
I wish to.

POLLIONE
How?

NORMA

                M'odi.
Pel tuo dio, pei figli tuoi,
giurar déi che d'ora in poi
Adalgisa fuggirai,
all'altar non la torrai…
e la vita io ti perdono
e mai più ti rivedrò.
Giura.

POLLIONE

        No: sì vil non sono.

NORMA *(con furore represso)*
Giura, giura!

POLLIONE *(con forza)*

          Ah! pria morrei!

NORMA
Non sai tu che il mio furore
passa il tuo?

POLLIONE

          Ch'ei piombi attendo.

NORMA
Non sai tu che ai figli in core
questo ferro…

POLLIONE *(con grido)*

          Oh! Dio, che intendo?

NORMA *(con pianto lacerante)*
Sì, sovr'essi alzai la punta…
Vedi… vedi a che son giunta!…
Non ferii… ma tosto… adesso
consumar potrei l'eccesso…
Un istante… e d'esser madre
mi poss'io dimenticar.

NORMA

Listen to me.
You must swear by your god
and your children that from this day on
you will shun Adalgisa,
that you will not take her from the altar;
then I shall spare your life
and never see you again.
Swear it.

POLLIONE

No, I am not so cowardly.

NORMA *(holding back her anger)*
Swear it, swear it!

POLLIONE *(vehemently)*
I'd sooner die.

NORMA

Do you not know that my anger
is greater than yours?

POLLIONE

I wait for it to be unleashed.

NORMA

Do you not know that into your children's hearts
this blade...

POLLIONE *(crying out)*
Oh, God! What am I hearing?

NORMA *(weeping bitterly)*
Yes, I raised the blade above them.
Do you see what I have been brought to?
I did not strike, but now I could soon
carry out the deed.
For a moment I could forget
that I was a mother.

POLLIONE
>Ah! crudele! in sen del padre
>il pugnal tu déi vibrar.
>A me il porgi.

NORMA
>> A te!

POLLIONE
>>> Che spento
>cada io solo!

NORMA
>> Solo?... Tutti.
>I romani a cento a cento
>fian mietuti, fian distrutti...
>E Adalgisa...

POLLIONE
>> Ahimè!

NORMA
>>> Infedele
>a' suoi voti...

POLLIONE
>> Ebben, crudele?

NORMA (con furore)
>Adalgisa fia punita;
>nelle fiamme perirà.

POLLIONE
>Ah! ti prendi la mia vita,
>ma di lei, di lei pietà.

NORMA
>Preghi alfine? Indegno! è tardi.
>Nel suo cor ti vo' ferire.
>Già mi pasco ne' tuoi sguardi,
>del tuo duol, del suo morire:

POLLIONE

Oh, cruel woman, it is into their father's breast
that you should plunge the knife.
Strike me.

NORMA

You!

POLLIONE

So that I alone
may die!

NORMA

Alone! All of you.
Let hundreds upon hundreds of Romans
be cut down, be destroyed.
And Adalgisa...

POLLIONE

Alas!

NORMA

She has broken
her vows...

POLLIONE

Well, you cruel woman?

NORMA *(furiously)*

Adalgisa must be punished.
She will perish in the flames.

POLLIONE

Oh, take away my life,
but have pity on her.

NORMA

Are you begging at last? You contemptible man. It's too late.
I shall wound you through her heart.
Already I take pleasure in the look you give me,
in your grief and in her death;

posso alfine, io posso farti
infelice al par di me.

POLLIONE
Ah! t'appaghi il mio terrore;
al tuo piè son io piangente…
In me sfoga il tuo furore,
ma risparmia un'innocente:
basti, basti a vendicarti
ch'io mi sveni innanzi a te.
Dammi quel ferro.

NORMA
                    Che osi?
Scostati.

POLLIONE
            Il ferro, il ferro!

NORMA
                        Olà, ministri,
sacerdoti, accorrete.

Scena XI

(Ritornano Oroveso, i Druidi, i Bardi e i Guerrieri.)

NORMA
                    All'ira vostra
nuova vittima io svelo. Una spergiura
sacerdotessa i sacri voti infranse,
tradì la patria, e il dio degli avi offese.

OROVESO, DRUIDI, SACERDOTESSE
Oh, delitto! oh, furor! La fa' palese.

NORMA
Sì, preparate il rogo.

POLLIONE *(a Norma)*
                    Oh! Ancor ti prego…
Norma, pietà.

at last I can make you
as miserable as I am.

POLLIONE

Oh, let my fear be enough for you;
I weep at your feet.
Pour out all your anger on me
but save an innocent girl.
Let it satisfy your vengeance
that I die in front of you.
Give me that knife.

NORMA

What do you mean to do?
Away!

POLLIONE

The knife.

NORMA

Priests,
attendants, come here.

Scene 11

(Oroveso and the Druids, Bards and Warriors all return.)

NORMA

I can reveal a new victim
for your anger. A deceitful priestess
has broken her vows,
betrayed her country and offended the god of our ancestors.

OROVESO, DRUIDS, PRIESTESSES

What a crime! What anger! Reveal her.

NORMA

Yes, make ready the pyre.

POLLIONE *(to Norma)*

Oh, I beg you once more,
Norma, have pity.

OROVESO, DRUIDI, SACERDOTESSE
La svela.

NORMA
Udite... (Io rea
l'innocente accusar del fallo mio?)

OROVESO, DRUIDI, SACERDOTESSE
Parla: chi è dessa?

POLLIONE *(a Norma)*
Ah! non lo dir.

NORMA
Son io.

OROVESO, DRUIDI, SACERDOTESSE
Tu!... Norma!...

NORMA
Io stessa. Il rogo ergete.

OROVESO, DRUIDI, SACERDOTESSE
(D'orror io gelo).

POLLIONE
(Mi manca il cor).

OROVESO, DRUIDI, SACERDOTESSE
Tu delinquente!

POLLIONE
Non le credete.

NORMA
Norma non mente.

OROVESO
Oh! mio rossor!

DRUIDI, SACERDOTESSE
Oh! quale orror!...

OROVESO, DRUIDS, PRIESTESSES
Expose her.

NORMA

Listen. (When I am guilty,
how can I accuse an innocent girl of my sin?)

OROVESO, DRUIDS, PRIESTESSES
Tell us, who is she?

POLLIONE *(to Norma)*
Oh, don't say it.

NORMA

It is I.

OROVESO, DRUIDS, PRIESTESSES
You! Norma!

NORMA

Myself. Build up the pyre.

OROVESO, DRUIDS, PRIESTESSES
(I'm frozen with horror.)

POLLIONE

(My heart has stopped beating.)

OROVESO, DRUIDS, PRIESTESSES
You, a criminal!

POLLIONE

Do not believe her.

NORMA
Norma does not lie.

OROVESO

Oh, my shame.

DRUIDS, PRIESTESSES
How terrible!

NORMA *(a Pollione)*
   Qual cor tradisti, qual cor perdesti   [26]
   quest'ora orrenda ti manifesti.
   Da me fuggire tentasti invano;
   crudel romano, tu sei con me.
   Un nume, un fato di te più forte
   ci vuole uniti in vita e in morte.
   Sul rogo istesso che mi divora,
   sotterra ancora sarò con te.

POLLIONE *(a Norma)*
   Ah! troppo tardi t'ho conosciuta,
   sublime donna, io t'ho perduta…
   Col mio rimorso è amor rinato,
   più disperato, furente egli è.
   Moriamo assieme, ah! sì, moriamo;
   l'estremo accento sarà ch'io t'amo.
   Ma tu, morendo, non m'abborrire,
   pria di morire perdona a me.

OROVESO, DRUIDI, SACERDOTESSE
   Oh! in te ritorna, ci rassicura;
   canuto padre te ne scongiura:
   di' che deliri, di' che tu menti,
   che stolti accenti uscir da te.
   Il dio severo che qui t'intende
   se stassi muto, se il tuon sospende,
   indizio è questo, indizio espresso
   che tanto eccesso punir non de'.

NORMA *(ai Sacerdoti)*
   Io son la rea…

POLLIONE *(accostandosi a Norma)*
   Non m'abborrire.

NORMA *(a Pollione)*
   Qual cor perdesti,
   quest'ora orrenda tel dica.

NORMA *(to Pollione)*

May this terrible moment now show you [26]
the heart you betrayed and lost.
You tried in vain to leave me,
and now you are with me, cruel Roman.
There is a god and a destiny stronger than you
that wishes us to be together in life and in death.
On the very pyre which will consume me
and in the grave I shall be with you still.

POLLIONE *(to Norma)*

Alas, I have come to know you too late,
you are a wonderful woman, and now I have lost you.
My love has been reborn with my remorse,
more despairing and angry.
Let us die together,
my last words will be, 'I love you'.
But as you die, do not look on me with loathing,
before you die, forgive me.

OROVESO, DRUIDS, PRIESTESSES

Come to your senses, reassure us;
your aged father is begging you:
tell us you are raving, tell us you are lying,
that what you are saying is foolishness.
If the stern god who hears you
is silent and withholds his thunder,
then this is a clear sign
that this crime should not be punished.

NORMA *(to the Priests)*

I am the guilty one.

POLLIONE *(joining Norma)*

Do not loathe me.

NORMA *(to Pollione)*

May this terrible moment show you
the heart that you have lost.

POLLIONE
Moriamo insieme.
Ah! sì, moriam.
Ah! perdona. Ah! t'ho perduta!

NORMA
Sì, e per sempre.
Quest'ora orrenda tel dica.

OROVESO, DRUIDI, SACERDOTESSE
Norma!... Deh! Norma, scolpati.
Taci?... ne ascolti appena?

NORMA *(a Pollione, che solo sente le sue parole; scuotendosi)*
Cielo! e i miei figli?

POLLIONE
          Ahi! miseri!

NORMA *(volgendosi a Pollione)*
I nostri figli?

POLLIONE
          Oh pena!

(Norma, come colpita da un'idea, s'incammina verso il padre. Pollione in tutta questa scena osserverà con agitazione i movimenti di Norma e Oroveso.)

OROVESO, DRUIDI, SACERDOTESSE
Norma, sei rea?

NORMA
          Sì, rea
oltre ogni umana idea.

OROVESO, DRUIDI, SACERDOTESSE
Empia!

NORMA *(ad Oroveso)*
          Tu m'odi?

POLLIONE
Let us die together.
Ah, yes, let us die.
Oh, forgive me! Oh, I have lost you.

NORMA
Yes, and for ever.
Let this terrible moment show you.

OROVESO, DRUIDS, PRIESTESSES
Norma, vindicate yourself.
You say nothing? Are you even listening?

NORMA *(to Pollione, who is the only one to hear her; coming to)*
Heavens! What about my children?

POLLIONE
Alas, the poor little ones!

NORMA *(turning to Pollione)*
Our children?

POLLIONE
Oh, sorrow!

(Suddenly Norma goes towards her father, as if struck by a thought. Pollione, throughout the scene that follows, agitatedly watches the exchange between Norma and Oroveso.)

OROVESO, DRUIDS, PRIESTESSES
Norma, are you guilty?

NORMA
Yes, more guilty
than you could imagine.

OROVESO, DRUIDS, PRIESTESSES
Sinful woman!

NORMA *(to Oroveso)*
Will you listen to me?

OROVESO

Scostati.

NORMA *(a stento trascinandolo in disparte)*
Deh! m'odi!

OROVESO

Oh! mio dolor!

NORMA *(piano ad Oroveso)*
Son madre...

OROVESO *(colpito)*
Madre!

NORMA

Acquetati...
Clotilde... ha i figli miei...
Tu li raccogli... e ai barbari
gl'invola insiem con lei...

OROVESO
No, giammai: va', lasciami.

NORMA
Ah! padre!... un prego ancor.

(S'inginocchia.)

OROVESO, POLLIONE
Oh! mio dolor!

DRUIDI, SACERDOTESSE
Oh! qual orror!...

NORMA *(sempre piano ad Oroveso)*
Deh! non volerli vittime
del mio fatale errore...
Deh! non troncar sul fiore
quell'innocente età.
Pensa che son tuo sangue...
abbi di lor pietà,

[27]

OROVESO

Away.

NORMA *(dragging him to one side)*
Please, listen to me!

OROVESO

Oh, my sorrow!

NORMA *(quietly, to Oroveso)*
I am a mother.

OROVESO *(stunned)*
A mother!

NORMA

Be calm.
Clotilde has my children.
Go and collect them, and with her
hide them from the barbarians.

OROVESO
No, never. Go away, leave me.

NORMA
Oh, father! One last request.

(She kneels.)

OROVESO, POLLIONE
Oh, my sorrow!

DRUIDS, PRIESTESSES
What horror!

NORMA *(quietly to Oroveso)*
Please don't make them suffer   [27]
for my heinous crime.
Please don't cut them down
in the flower of their youth.
Remember that they are your blood,
have mercy on them,

ah! padre,
abbi di lor pietà.

POLLIONE

Commosso è già.

DRUIDI, SACERDOTESSE

Piange!... prega!... che mai spera?
Qui respinta è la preghiera.
Le si spogli il crin dal serto:
la si copra di squallor.

NORMA

Padre! tu piangi?

OROVESO

Oppresso è il core.

NORMA

Piangi e perdona.

OROVESO

Ha vinto amore,
oh ciel! ah sì!

POLLIONE

Oh ciel! ah sì!

NORMA

Ah! tu perdoni. Quel pianto il dice.
Io più non chiedo. Io son felice.

OROVESO

Oh duol! Figlia!...

NORMA

Ah! più non chiedo.
Contenta il rogo io ascenderò.

POLLIONE

Ah! più non chiedo.
Contento il rogo io ascenderò.

oh, father,
have mercy on them.

POLLIONE

Now he is moved.

DRUIDS, PRIESTESSES
She is weeping, praying. What is she hoping for?
Her prayer will be rejected.
Let the wreath be taken from her brow
and her head be veiled.

NORMA
Are you crying, father?

OROVESO

My heart is heavy.

NORMA
Cry and forgive.

OROVESO

Love has conquered,
oh Heavens! Ah, yes!

POLLIONE
Oh Heavens! Ah, yes!

NORMA
Oh, you forgive. Your tears tell me.
I ask for nothing more. I am content.

OROVESO
What sorrow! My daughter...

NORMA

I ask for nothing more.
I shall happily mount the pyre.

POLLIONE

I ask for nothing more.
I shall happily mount the pyre.

OROVESO
Ah! consolarmi mai non potrò.

DRUIDI, SACERDOTESSE
Sì, piange! che mai spera?
Qui respinta è la preghiera.
Le si spogli il crin dal serto:
sia coperta di squallor.

POLLIONE
Più non chiedo, oh ciel! *ecc.*

NORMA
Padre, ah padre!

OROVESO
Ah! cessa, infelice!

NORMA
Tu mel prometti?...

OROVESO
Io tel prometto, ah sì!

NORMA
Ah! tu perdoni. Quel pianto il dice, *ecc.*

OROVESO
Ah sì! Oh duol! Figlia! *ecc.*

POLLIONE
Ah sì! Oh ciel! *ecc.*

(I Druidi coprono d'un velo nero la Sacerdotessa.)

DRUIDI, SACERDOTESSE
Vanne al rogo; ed il tuo scempio
purghi l'ara e lavi il tempio,
maledetta estinta ancor!

OROVESO
Va', infelice!

OROVESO
Oh, I shall never be consoled.

DRUIDS, PRIESTESSES
Yes, she is weeping. What is she hoping for?
Her prayer will be rejected.
Let the wreath be taken from her brow,
and her head be veiled.

POLLIONE
Heavens, I ask for nothing more, *etc.*

NORMA
Father!

OROVESO
Enough, you poor girl!

NORMA
Do you promise me?

OROVESO
I promise, ah, yes!

NORMA
Oh, you forgive me. Your tears tell me, *etc.*

OROVESO
Ah, yes! What sorrow! My daughter, *etc.*

POLLIONE
Ah, yes! Oh, heavens, *etc.*

(The Druids cover Norma in a black veil.)

DRUIDS, PRIESTESSES
Go to the pyre; and may your death
purge the altar and cleanse the temple,
woman accursed even in death.

OROVESO
Go, unhappy girl!

NORMA *(incamminandosi)*
      Padre!... addio.

POLLIONE
  Il tuo rogo, o Norma, è il mio.
  Là più puro, là più santo
  incomincia eterno amor.

NORMA *(volgendosi ancora una volta)*
  Padre!... addio!...

OROVESO *(la guarda)*
  Sgorga alfin, prorompi, o pianto,
  sei permesso a un genitor.

NORMA *(as she begins walking towards the pyre)*
Farewell, father!

POLLIONE
Norma, your pyre is mine as well.
There a purer, holier,
everlasting love will begin.

NORMA *(turning once more)*
Farewell, father!...

OROVESO *(gazing at her)*
Flow, at last, my tears:
tears are a father's right.

Select Discography

There is no complete up-to-date discussion in English or discography of the recordings available. http://www.operadis-opera-discography. org.uk/CLBLNORM.HTM lists 119 complete audio performances, including transfers of many 'off-the-air' broadcasts, up until 2008. For discussions of selected recordings up to 1979, see Andrew Porter, '*Norma*', *Opera on Record*, ed. Alan Blyth (London: Hutchinson, 1979), pp. 154–72 and, up to 1993, Roland Graeme, '*Norma*', *The Metropolitan Opera Guide to Recorded Opera*, ed. Paul Gruber (London and New York: Thames and Hudson, 1993), pp. 21–8.

This selection highlights some of the leading interpretations. Of the two studio versions featuring Maria Callas (1954 and 1960), there is still considerable debate as to which is to be preferred. Of the three live Callas recordings listed here, the 1955 RAI Symphony version is perhaps the most satisfying, while the 1952 Royal Opera House version has the young Joan Sutherland as Clotilde.

YEAR	CAST	CONDUCTOR/ORCHESTRA/ CHORUS	LABEL
	Norma		
	Pollione		
	Adalgisa		
	Oroveso		
	Flavio		
	Clotilde		
1937*	Gina Cigna	Vittorio Gui	Premiere
	Giovanni Breviaro	EIAR Symphony	Opera
	Ebe Stignani	Orchestra Turin and Chorus	(live)
	Tancredo Pasero		
	Emilio Renzi		
	Adriana Perris		

1952*	Maria Callas Mirto Picchi Ebe Stignani Giacomo Vaghi Paul Asciak Joan Sutherland	Vittorio Gui Royal Opera House Orchestra and Chorus	Warner (live)
1954*	Maria Callas Mario Filippeschi Ebe Stignani Nicola Rossi-Lemeni Paolo Caroli Rina Cavallari	Tullio Serafin La Scala Orchestra and Chorus	Warner
1955*	Maria Callas Mario Del Monaco Ebe Stignani Giuseppe Modesti Athos Cesarina Rina Cavallari	Tullio Serafin RAI Symphony Orchestra Rome and Chorus	Myto (live)
1955*	Maria Callas Mario Del Monaco Giulietta Simionato Nicola Zaccaria Giuseppe Zampieri Gabriella Carturan	Antonino Votto La Scala Orchestra and Chorus	Myto (live)
1960	Maria Callas Franco Corelli Christa Ludwig Nicola Zaccaria Piero De Palma Edda Vincenzi	Tullio Serafin La Scala Orchestra and Chorus	Warner
1964	Joan Sutherland John Alexander Marilyn Horne Richard Cross Joseph Ward Yvonne Minton	Richard Bonynge LSO and Chorus	Decca

1972	Montserrat Caballé Plácido Domingo Fiorenza Cossotto Ruggero Raimondi Kenneth Collins Elizabeth Bainbridge	Carlo Felice Cillario London Philharmonic, Ambrosian Opera Chorus	RCA Victor
1973	Beverly Sills Enrico Di Giuseppe Shirley Verrett Paul Plishka Robert Tear Delia Wallis	James Levine New Philharmonia John Alldis Choir	DG
1979	Renato Scotto Giuseppe Giacomini Tatiana Troyanos Paul Plishka Paul Crook Ann Murray	James Levine National Philharmonic Ambrosian Opera Chorus	Sony
1984	Joan Sutherland Luciano Pavarotti Montserrat Caballé Samuel Ramey Kim Begley Diana Montague	Richard Bonynge Welsh National Opera and Chorus	Decca
1994	Jane Eaglen Vincenzo La Scola Eva Mei Dimitri Kavrakos Ernesto Gavazzini Carmela Remigio	Riccardo Muti Maggio Musicale Fiorentino and Chorus	Warner (live)
2004	Edita Gruberová Aquiles Machado Elīna Garanča Alastair Miles Ray M. Wade Judith Howarth	Friedrich Haider Staatsphilharmonie Rheinland-Pfalz Vocal Ensemble Rastatt	Nightingale

| 2013 | Cecilia Bartoli
John Osborn
Sumi Jo
Michele Pertusi
Reinaldo Macias
Liliana Nikiteanu | Giovanni Antonini
La Scintilla, Zurich
International Chamber
Vocalists | Decca
(New critical
edition
by Maurizio
Biondi and
Riccardo
Minasi)
(played on
period
instruments) |

* mono

Norma on DVD

There is no complete up-to-date discussion in English of *Norma* on DVD available in English. http://www.operadis-opera-discography. org.uk/CLBLNORM.HTM lists thirteen DVD recordings of productions up until 2008. An annotated list up to 2003 – including early and related films, both commercially released and otherwise – may be found in Ken Wlaschin, *Encyclopedia of Opera on Screen* (Yale 2004), pp. 492–94.

This selection highlights some of the leading interpretations.

YEAR	CAST Norma Pollione Adalgisa Oroveso Flavio Clotilde	CONDUCTOR/ORCHESTRA/ CHORUS	DIRECTOR/ COMPANY/ LABEL
1974	Montserrat Caballé Jon Vickers Josephine Veasey Agostino Ferrin Gino Sinimberghi Marisa Zotti	Giuseppe Patané Teatro Regio, Turin and Chorus	Sandro Sequi Teatro Regio, Turin Hardy
1978	Joan Sutherland Ronald Stevens Margreta Elkins Clifford Grant Trevor Brown Etela Piha	Richard Bonynge Elizabethan Sydney Orchestra and Australian Opera Chorus	Sandro Sequi Australian Opera, Sydney Arthaus Musik

1981	Joan Sutherland Francisco Ortiz Tatiana Troyanos Justino Díaz Michael Shust Frances Ginze	Richard Bonynge Canadian Opera Company and Chorus	Lotfi Mansouri Canadian Opera VAI
2001	June Anderson Shin Young Hoon Daniela Barcellona Ildar Abdrazakov Leonardo Melani Svetlana Ignatovitch	Fabio Biondi Europa Galante and Verdi Festival Chorus	Roberto Andò Teatro Regio, Parma TDK (played on period instruments)
2005	Dimitra Theodossiou Carlo Ventre Nidia Palacios Ricardo Zanellato Mariano Brischetto Maria Grazia Calderone	Giuliano Carella Teatro Massimo Bellini di Catania and Chorus	Walter Pagliaro Teatro Massimo Bellini di Catania Dynamic
2005	Hasmik Papian Hugh Smith Irini Tsirakidis Giorgio Giuseppia Carlo Bosi Anna Steiger	Julian Reynolds Nederlands Kammerorkest and Chorus	Guy Joosten Het Muziektheater, Amsterdam Opus Arte
2006	Edita Gruberová Zoran Todorović Sonia Ganassi Roberto Scandiuzzi Markus Herzog Cynthia Jansen	Friedrich Haider Bavarian State Opera and Chorus	Jürgen Rose Bavarian State Opera DG
2007	Fiorenza Cedolins Vincenzo La Scola Sonia Ganassi Andrea Papi Jon Plazaola Begoña Alberdi	Giuliano Carella Gran Teatro del Liceu and Chorus	Francisco Negrin Gran Teatro del Liceu Arthaus Musik

Select Bibliography

Ardoin, John, *The Callas Legacy: The Complete Guide to Her Recordings on Compact Discs* (London: Duckworth, 4th edition, 1995)

Galatopoulos, Stelios, *Bellini: Life, Times, Music, 1801–1835* (London: Sanctuary, 2002)

Galatopoulos, Stelios, *Maria Callas: Sacred Monster* (London: Fourth Estate, 1998)

Kimbell, David, *Italian Opera* (Cambridge: Cambridge University Press, 1991)

Kimbell, David, *Vincenzo Bellini: Norma* (Cambridge: Cambridge University Press, 1998)

Maguire, Simon, *Vincenzo Bellini and the Aesthetics of Early Nineteenth-Century Italian Opera* (New York: Garland, 1989)

Orrey, Leslie, *Bellini* (London: Dent, 1969)

Rosen, Charles, *The Romantic Generation* (Cambridge, MA: Harvard University Press, 1995)

Rosselli, John, *The Life of Bellini* (Cambridge: Cambridge University Press, 1996)

Weinstock, Herbert, *Vincenzo Bellini: His Life and His Operas* (London: Weidenfeld and Nicolson, 1972)

Willier, Stephen A., *Vincenzo Bellini: A Research and Information Guide* (New York and London: Routledge, 2nd edition, 2009)

Bellini Websites*

In English or with an English-language option

List of stage works   *www.opera.stanford.edu/Bellini*

Norma discography and DVD listing

         www.operadis-opera-discography.org.uk/CLBLNORM.HTM

Fondazione Bellini, Universitá di Catania   *www.studibelliniani.eu*

In Italian

Bellini News   *www.bellininews.it*

* Links valid at the time of publication in 2016.

Note on the Contributors

John Allison is editor of *Opera* magazine and music critic of the *Daily Telegraph*. He was born in South Africa and completed his PhD while playing the organ at Cape Town cathedral. He has written for publications around the world, authored books, contributed chapters to several volumes and served on the juries of many international singing competitions.

Kenneth Chalmers is a translator and writer on music. He has translated numerous opera libretti and is Head of Surtitles at the Royal Opera House. His translations include the final volume of Lorenzo Bianconi and Giorgio Pestelli's *The History of Italian Opera* (Chicago University Press, 2004) and Constantin Floros's *New Ears for New Music* (Peter Lang, 2014).

Gary Kahn has been series editor of the Overture/ENO opera guides since 2010. He has previously worked for BBC Television and English National Opera. He is currently a freelance dramaturg. His book *The Power of the Ring* was published by the Royal Opera House in 2007 and reissued in a revised edition in 2012.

Roger Parker is Professor of Music at King's College London. He is General Editor (with Gabriele Dotto) of the Donizetti critical edition, published by Ricordi. His most recent book is *A History of Opera: The Last Four Hundred Years* (Allen Lane, 2012), written jointly with Carolyn Abbate. His critical edition of *Norma*, now in preparation, will be published by Ricordi.

Susan Rutherford is Senior Lecturer in Music at the University of Manchester. Her publications include *The Prima Donna and Opera*, *1815–1930* (Cambridge University Press, 2006) and *Verdi, Opera, Women* (Cambridge University Press, 2013), as well as numerous essays on the history of voice, performance, and nineteenth-century opera.

Acknowledgements

We would like to thank John Allison of *Opera*, Charles Johnston, Mike Ashman and George Hall for their assistance and advice in the preparation of this guide and Robin Gordon-Powell for his setting of the music examples in the Thematic Guide. Giovanni Pasqualino of *Bellini News* and Stephen A. Willier of Temple University, Philadelphia, have also contributed expert guidance. John Pennino of the Metropolitan Opera Archives, Mike Markiewicz of ArenaPAL and the Museo Teatrale alla Scala generously helped provide photographs.

www.overturepublishing.com
www.eno.org